SETTING THE AGENDA

SETTING THE AGENDA

The Report of the 1999 Church of England
Conference on Evangelism
ACE '99

8 –12 March 1999

Board of Mission Occasional Paper No. 10

CHURCH HOUSE
PUBLISHING

BV
3777
.G7
S47
1999

Church House Publishing
Church House
Great Smith Street
London
SW1P 3NZ

ISBN 0 7151 5545 8

Published 1999 for the Board of Mission of the Church of England by Church House Publishing

© *The Archbishops' Council* 1999

This report has only the authority of the Board of Mission of the Church of England for which it was produced.

Cover design and illustration by Julian Smith
Printed in England by Halstan & Co. Ltd

Contents

Contents

Introduction

ACE '99 was a unique gathering. Representatives came from every diocese in the Church of England, from our ecumenical partners and from selected voluntary agencies. The spread of backgrounds and perspectives represented the diversity to be found amongst all the Churches at this time. That such groups were present was proof enough of the effect that the Decade of Evangelism has had upon the Churches. People and groups who, ten years ago, would not have expressed any particular interest in evangelism were present at ACE '99. The Churches as a whole have embraced and want to obey God's call to express the love of God in the world. What became clear at the conclusion of ACE '99 was that the journey begun by the Decade of Evangelism is not over. The Churches still have a long way to go. We have heard God's call but still have much to learn and far to travel in the journey of becoming God's missionary communities.

The purpose of ACE '99 was to reflect on what the Churches have learnt during the Decade of Evangelism and to seek God's equipping and enabling as we move into the new Millennium. What became apparent during ACE '99 was that the conference was only the beginning of this process. It was a milestone on the way, not the end of the journey. The process of reflecting and analysing what we have learnt and looking forward to the future is one for the whole Church and not simply for a one-off conference. The conference provided the necessary stimulus but is not the end. This report is provided to help this process and to enable those who were not at ACE '99 to take part in this journey.

This report is an attempt to disseminate to the wider Church the contributions and findings from ACE '99 so that we can all join in this process of finding God's way for the future.

Conference Process

Participants

In 1997 invitations were sent to all Diocesan Bishops of the Church of England asking them to send four delegates to take part in the 1999 Church of England Conference on Evangelism which came to be known as ACE '99. Bishops were asked to send one representative under 30, two from parish level and one from the diocesan structures.

At the same time invitations were sent to all the major denominations in England as well as to ecumenical bodies in Wales, Scotland and Ireland. In addition invitations were issued to voluntary agencies who are members of Partnership for World Mission as well as to those whose main work is evangelism. These bodies were invited to send participants on a basis similar to that set out for the Church of England dioceses.

The full involvement of our ecumenical partners was thought by the Steering Group to be strategic. To this end it was decided that there would be no division between full participants and ecumenical observers. Those representing other denominations would be full participants in ACE '99 and as such would take a full part in the leadership of the conference. In the event 35 participants (one-sixth of the whole conference) were representatives of the major denominations. This figure could have been higher but some denominations were not able to fill their full allocation of places. Of the speakers at the Plenary Sessions three were from denominations other than the Church of England. One member of the Steering Group is a Minister of the United Reformed Church and Co-ordinating Secretary of the Churches Together in England Group for Evangelization. Ecumenical participants were also involved in leading Base Groups and Tracks as well as in chairing Plenary Sessions. Whilst the majority of participants were representatives from the dioceses of the Church of England those from other denominations as well as from the voluntary agencies were fully involved in the leadership of the conference.

Making preparations

The process of ACE '99 began well before the first day of the conference. Before the conference, participants were asked to undertake a series of four studies to prepare for ACE '99. The four main questions participants were asked to address were:

● What have you learnt so far in the Decade of Evangelism?

● What has worked and not worked in the Decade?

● What is this showing for the future?

● What issues would you like to see addressed at the conference?

These questions were addressed in the context of Bible study on the parables in Matthew chapter 13. Delegates were also asked to do research in their own diocese, denomination or voluntary agency using the four questions and, if possible, make a presentation of the group's findings to key decision makers in their constituency.

Those groups who worked with this material found it stimulating. However, many of those attending ACE '99 were unable to do this work in time for the conference. A summary of the responses is contained in Chapter 1 of this report. This provides a valuable beginning to the work of reflecting upon and assessing the Decade.

Conference process

ACE '99 was structured around four programmes or levels. They were the Plenary Programme, the Tracks Programme, the Base Group Programme and the Special Interest Seminar Programme. Each level had a different purpose though each was equally valid as part of the whole process of the conference. The conference was jointly chaired by the Bishops of Southwark and Wakefield.

The *Plenary Programme* consisted of ten gatherings of the whole conference to hear speakers such as the Archbishop of Canterbury, Paul Vallely, Revd Rose Hudson-Wilkin, Bishop Lindsay Urwin, Bishop Henri Orombi and John and Olive Drane. The Tracks and Base Group Programmes also reported to the whole conference in plenary. The purpose of these presentations was to inspire and envision the conference members and through them the Churches. The texts of the plenary talks are found in Chapter 2 of this report.

The *Tracks Programme* was designed to equip participants with the vision, ideas and skills to carry evangelism into the new millennium. The sessions were practical, concerned to listen and use the experience of participants as well as the leader and to be future-orientated. Issues addressed in the Tracks sessions were: Children and Evangelism, Arts and Evangelism, Process Evangelism, Women in Evangelism, Spirituality – the Heart of Evangelism, the World Church and Evangelism in England, Reaching Men in Millennium 3, Transforming the Local Church in Mission, Practising

Good News to the Poor, Making the Most of the Millennium, Youth and Evangelism, and Equipping the Church to Tell God's Story. Some Tracks met three times for a total of six hours and others met twice for a total of four hours.

The *Base Groups* were designed to provide a small unit of belonging through which participants could reflect and raise questions about issues emerging at ACE '99 and beyond. Groups consisted of between eight and twelve people. Evaluation forms showed that for many people the Base Groups were the most exciting part of the conference with a lively exchange of views in a safe atmosphere.

The *Special Interest Seminars* provided an opportunity for participants to consider further some of the current issues and initiatives in evangelism. They were an opportunity to draw on some of the experience and expertise of the many voluntary organizations who work in evangelism. Subjects covered include Reaching out to Families, The Alpha Course, Church Planting, Evangelistic Preaching, Cringe-Free Evangelism, Images of Christ from the World Church, Evangelism in a Nervous Church, Natural Church Development, Cell Church, Groundswell, Young People in Evangelism and Small Churches in Rural Areas.

1

On the Road to ACE '99

Summary of Responses
to 'Making Preparations'

Delegates to ACE '99 were asked to work through a short programme of study, prayer and discussion entitled 'Making Preparations'. This summary seeks to reflect and bring together the responses that have been received. Responses have been received from 22 dioceses, 2 denominations and 13 voluntary agencies. Participants were asked to address four main questions:

- What have you learnt so far in the Decade of Evangelism?

- What has worked and not worked in the Decade?

- What is this showing for the future?

- What issues should be addressed at the conference?

This summary follows these four main questions.

What have you learnt so far in the Decade of Evangelism?

- **There has been a major shift in attitude towards evangelism during the Decade**

    The majority of responses reported that there had been a major shift in the way the Churches perceived evangelism during the Decade. Those dioceses who sent out questionnaires to parishes as part of their response report a favourable response rate and that parishes reported that they had been challenged during the Decade in their attitudes towards mission and evangelism and had learnt much as a result. What was proving to be more difficult is to translate the shift in attitude into action. Mission and evangelism are increasingly becoming an integral part of both clergy and lay training at all levels. During the Decade many churches have realized the integral place of mission and evangelism in the life and purpose of the Church.

- **Relationships are the key to effective evangelism**

    Finding Faith Today, published in 1992, clearly pointed the way towards effective evangelism being based on relationships. The results of the research which formed the basis for Finding Faith Today

3

has been confirmed by experience in the rest of the Decade. Relationships which are effective in evangelism are characterized by love, care and witness. This realization has given rise to a growth in resources which provide a vehicle for learning about the Christian faith in the context of relationships.

● **A variety of approaches to evangelism are necessary**

There is no single approach or resource that is applicable in every situation. Where published resources are used they need adaptation to different contexts. Published resources are valuable in providing models for mission and evangelism but where churches adapt material to local needs evangelism is most effective.

● **Action and proclamation go hand in hand**

Action and proclamation are not separate activities. They exist together in the presentation of the gospel of Jesus Christ to a broken world. Action and proclamation are two sides of the same coin.

● **Evangelism is tough, hard work and requires patience and constant evaluation and re-evaluation**

Few of the responses stated explicitly the results they had seen from evangelism during the Decade. This perhaps points us to the reality that evangelism is not a quick-fix solution to a decline in church numbers but a long-term commitment on the part of the Church to follow God in his saving love into the world. In order to learn it is necessary to evaluate so that it is important that the Church develops a pattern for action, reflection, evaluation and further action.

● **Spirituality is at the heart of evangelism**

The desire to evangelize finds its roots in a relationship with God. This is true for individual Christians as it is for churches. Without this, evangelism is empty. The love of God is the reason we evangelize. Together with this is the realization that the Holy Spirit is the evangelist and we are co-workers. Evangelism is not so much going out for God as following the Holy Spirit.

● **Evangelism cannot be isolated from other areas of church life such as ministry, worship and theology**

How we are church, how we worship and how we order our common life are all integral parts of our evangelism. The Decade has shown how all parts of church life are linked and bound together in the whole, under God the Holy Trinity. There is an urgent need to develop theological thinking on evangelism in the context of the whole life of the Church.

What has worked and what has not worked during the Decade?

● **The Occasional Offices are effective as a means of evangelism but opportunities coming through this route are fewer and fewer**

A number of responses stated that the Occasional Offices are an important way of doing evangelism in an Anglican style. However, this was balanced by the fact that opportunities are becoming fewer and fewer through this route and can no longer be relied on exclusively to provide opportunities for evangelism.

● **Initiatives that include community involvement work effectively as evangelism**

Activities such as mother and toddler groups, drop-in centres, after-school care, flower festivals etc. have become important vehicles for breaking down barriers between Church and community and opening up opportunities for evangelism. These are long-term projects that require commitment and focus. The majority of the responses reported that projects based on long-term presence evangelism were most effective.

● **Evangelism focused on special groups or projects has worked**

Examples are rural and urban evangelism, cell church, church planting, non-book culture, reaching out to men and women. The Decade has also stimulated much thought about what it means to be the Church in our culture.

- **Worship can work as effective evangelism**

  Worship is about experiencing the living God as well as the local Christian community. It is both upward and outward. Where worship contains both elements people are touched by the gospel.

- **Initiatives based on personal relationships have worked**

  Where initiatives and projects have emphasized and been based on relationship networks, evangelism has been effective and sustained. This has been true for events such as evangelistic missions as well as project-orientated evangelism in, for example, mother and toddler groups. Where this is not the case, evangelism has not been effective.

What is this showing for the future?

- **There is still the need to address the Sunday/Monday divide. How can the lives and witness of lay Christians working in the world be built and sustained?**

  For many Christians there is little link made between their lives in church and beyond into the everyday world. Yet, it is here that evangelism happens. There is a clear need for evangelism training to be focused in this area. The 'fringes' of Church life have often been seen to be fertile ground for evangelism. However, penetration beyond the fringe is difficult and long term. Many are asking the question as to how the Church reaches beyond the fringe. One key element in this movement is to equip lay Christians to live the Christian life beyond the boundaries of the Church. There is a need constantly to make and expand the fringe as contacts are developed.

- **How can churches adequately address the spiritual search of contemporary men and women?**

  The gap between Church and culture has been addressed in the Decade and will continue to need to be as we live in times of rapid change. Initiatives such as Building Missionary Congregations have given much attention to the interaction of church and contemporary cultures. We live in times where the language of spirituality is significant and popular. However, this is not necessarily Christian spirituality but often a 'pick and mix' from a variety of sources used as a vehicle for accessing a language of personal meaning. The Christian Church is no longer the only provider in spiritual matters. The market is open and competition is fierce.

● **Many churches are only just waking up to the need for evangelism – how can they be helped to move ahead?**

It is widely agreed that the calling of the Decade of Evangelism has seen a major change in attitude with regard to evangelism. However, there is a danger that this could be lost if, at the end of the Decade, the Church thinks 'we have done evangelism now' and goes back to what it was. Helping Christians to move ahead and build upon what has been learnt during the Decade is a major task but one which must be addressed urgently.

● **Key groups where the churches are not making an impact are children and youth and those in their thirties, forties and fifties.**

Many responding to Making Preparations agreed that the Church was making little impact with these groups. Some attention is being directed towards young people but children and thirties to fifties are not receiving the attention they warrant.

● **Visionary leadership is needed for the future**

Good leadership is one of the keys to the life of the Church. Leadership that encourages participation and inspires congregations to live out the love of God is vital as the Church develops into the new millennium.

What issues should be addressed at the conference?

The replies to this question were many and varied but here are some of the suggestions.

● Do we want to be kingdom people or church people?

● How can young people be heard if the Church doesn't listen?

● Develop approaches to evangelism that are linked with the human life cycle.

● Use Information Technology.

- Address the question of communication in a non-book world.

- Consider how to encourage smaller (rural and urban) churches in evangelism.

- Raise confidence in evangelism.

- How can we reach beyond the fringe?

- Spirituality (prayer and work) needs to dominate the conference.

- How do we keep evangelism on the agenda of the Church?

- What is the good news to the poorest areas?

- How should we approach a culture where increasing numbers have no Christian background or knowledge?

- Who will be accountable for dealing with resolutions from the conference?

- Recognize and value the role of the evangelist.

- How do we do evangelism ecumenically?

- Confront the problem of the upkeep of expensive church buildings and how this relates to evangelism.

- We hope ACE '99 will explore different theological understandings of evangelism.

Key quotations . . .

'There has certainly been more interest shown in evangelistic materials, and perhaps a little less reticence about asking for them. The most significant continuing interest has been in the Alpha and Emmaus courses.' (SPCK response)

'Church leaders are reflecting more on evangelism but the "now" is not being addressed.' (Liverpool Diocesan response)

'Effective evangelism is about people not structures . . . God's people themselves are the primary way in which the Gospel is shared through the ordinary events of life.' (Ripon Diocesan response)

'Undergirding the theme of evangelism there needs to be a clarifica-

tion of the theology of the people outside of Christ and a consequent commitment of compassion and prayer for such people.' (South American Missionary Society response)

'Kingdom people seek first the kingdom of God and its justice; church people often put church work above concerns for justice, mercy and truth. Church people think about how to get people into church; kingdom people think about how to get the Church into the world. Church people worry that the world might change the Church; kingdom people work to see the Church change in the world' (Durham Diocesan response)

'There still remains a considerable amount of antipathy towards mission and evangelism in many individuals and parishes which suggests that where the Decade has succeeded this has been primarily in those places where there was a pre-existing interest in and concern for faith sharing, outreach etc. There is a fear that once the Decade is over, many churches will simply opt to "return to type".' (Bath and Wells Diocesan response)

'We need the focus of evangelism to move away from the Church and to better equip Christians to witness where they are in daily life.' (Church Pastoral Aid Society response)

2

Plenary Presentations

Bible Readings

John and Olive Drane

Three Bible Readings were given combining expository and creative approaches. These summaries give a flavour of the presentations.

Bible Reading No. 1: Seeing the world the way God sees it – Acts 17

Paul at Athens (Acts 17). This is the pluralistic context in which we live and minister today: the supermarket of faiths or the spiritual market place where people searching for meaning, pick and choose from the many options before them. At the same time there is declining interest in religious institutions, and a massive rise in spiritual search.

Three lessons from Paul in Acts 17:

Listening before speaking – Paul was uneasy with some of what he saw and heard, but he went to see, to hear, to observe. He didn't speak at people but came alongside them. There are no no-go areas for God in today's spiritual search.

Journeying with others – altars to unknown gods. Paul did not sweep the altar to the unknown god away, but is seen as accepting and affirming the Athenians' starting points. Where are the altars to unknown gods – the spiritual starting points – in today's culture? There are many possible specific answers, and the altars to the unknown gods will be different in different communities. But historically we can see that certain broad issues have been important to different generations. For the Reformation the issue was guilt. For the Victorian era the big issue was death. Today it is meaning, healing and personal wholeness.

Faith is a process – don't expect instant results. Athens wasn't a failure, but an example of the cost of sharing faith. Jesus' teaching on taking up your cross, the first becoming last, foolishness versus wisdom is key to our understanding of evangelism today. Discipleship was never meant to be a bed of roses – but it is a challenge that is great enough and worthy enough to be worthwhile giving our lives to it. Evangelism involves taking risks and is tough.

So here are three questions we need to address urgently today.

● Where is God at work today?

● What are the unknown gods?

● Who are the Christians who will be bold enough to share faith courageously, and with God-inspired creativity?

An example of risky evangelism is the story of Ross Clifford, the Principal of Morling Theological College in Sydney, Australia. In his work in the theological college he thought that it was necessary to develop Christian ministers who could deal with the key questions that people were asking in today's culture. So he went to one of the altars of the unknown gods in Sydney – the psychic fair. He was particularly taken with the biblical imagery in the Tarot cards. He opened a stall at a future psychic fair and used this to explain the real meaning behind the Tarot cards. In this controversial method he used the cards to point searchers to the God of the Bible.

Bible Reading No. 2: Exploring new ways of being – Isaiah 11.1-10

Have you ever gone to the supermarket looking for something and not been able to find it – only to find it was there all along, but the package has been changed? For example, in Australia a Weetabix packet is blue not yellow. This shows how things change with context. One of the places we have visited during the Decade of Evangelism is Jamaica and we want to tell the story of Mount Zion Church in Jamaica. The strange thing about this church is that it is a Scottish church in the midst of Jamaica. It was brought from Glasgow in 1830 and built by slaves in their spare time (what little they were allowed). That church, transported from Scotland on empty boats, arrived not far from Rose Hall Plantation, which was owned by a woman called Annie Palmer who was thought of as half-human and half-devil. The church was constructed by slave labour because they were told that is what they had to do to serve Jesus Christ. On the day of the dedication of the church the people there were presented with a gift to mark their achievement in building it. The gift was a bell which would call them to worship. On the bell was inscribed the text from Corinthians – 'Where the Spirit of the Lord is there is freedom'. As we stood there in that place of so much exploitation we didn't know whether to laugh or cry. But as we say today 'the medium is the message' and few saw the discrepancy between medium and message in nineteenth-century Scotland or Jamaica.

Today this church is a situation with a bright future, and a dark history. It shows the contrasting styles of being Christian, and of inviting others to join us on the journey of faith, as between the original missionaries who took the church there, and those who now worship in it today.

What are some of the contrasting approaches this story shows?

- Mission easily becomes an exercise in conquest or marketing.

- Faith can be imposed from the top downwards – or grow from the bottom upwards.

- Faith that begins from an assumption that we own God – or mission that starts from a conviction that this is God's world, and therefore God must already be at work in it.

- Contrasting understandings of theology – one that thinks God is only to be found in the spaces where we feel comfortable, where we are in control – and another worldview that has no place for 'no-go areas' for God.

'The medium is the message' – our language and actions say something about the gospel – both positive and negative. The medium through which the message comes is very often the message that is received either commending, or distracting and devaluing.

Principles of God's kingdom (Isaiah 11)

So what should the medium be like? What does it mean for you and me to be God's agents in bringing in a better way of being? Three qualities stand out here:

Generosity (v.3) – generosity towards one another. God's agents for change 'will not judge by the way things look or decide by what we hear'. That is easy to say, much harder to do. So many of the world's problems are caused by looking at the externals, and missing what is really important about people. Old people look at young people, and dismiss them because they dress differently, behave differently, learn differently, have different expectations of what is possible. Young people look at old people and see their grey hair and stiff limbs and ask 'how can anyone like that possibly be cool?' Those whose lives are comfortable look at those who have hard times, whether economically, or as victims of violence or abuse, and easily say 'but she must have asked for it'. And it happens in the Church too, as someone uses different terminology than we might have used ourselves, and so we dismiss or discredit them as somehow being people of less faith than we are. Generosity – to ourselves as well as to others – will always be one of the underlying principles of God's way of doing things, God's kingdom.

Justice is another (vv. 4-5). To be part of God's kingdom is to recognize some absolute standards – in this case, of right and wrong, justice and injustice. What is fair and what is unfair. When today's Christians think of standards, they often imagine this has only to do with personal morality, and as a result the Church easily finds itself wrong-footed, supporting causes that lead to death and opposing causes that, in the grander story of human life, are actually part of the story of God's kingdom. I only have to mention things like the Crusades, the building of empire, slavery, the consistent marginalization of women, the undervaluing of children, for you to get the message.

Our tendency to major on individual morality, while ignoring the great social evils of our day, is one of the reasons why non-Christians so easily dismiss the Church as hypocritical. Nine times out of ten, when the Bible talks about morality, it is justice that is in the frame. And as I look at some of the great social issues of the moment, and contemplate Christian responses to and comments on them, there is no doubt that we are in danger of making the same mistakes as our forebears sometimes did.

Truth – Justice depends on truth. Actually, the key issues today as we engage in the struggle to be God's people and to be fully human, are more pressing than matters of personal morality. For what is it that will inspire and empower us not only to recognize God's will, but actually to do it? Verse 2 of our passage reveals that truth and wisdom come from God. We are at the end of a long period of history in which we have learned a lot of painful lessons. As we stand on the threshold of the twenty-first century, that question 'Would we recognize God's kingdom if we saw it?' is a very real one. For more and more insistently, the clamouring voices are telling us that there is nothing foundational and fundamental that is worth recognizing anyway. That any sense of searching for things of ultimate value that will resonate in the lives of all the world's people is a waste of time. That the best we can do is recognize our differences and live with the fragmentation that inevitably follows in a world where everything is reduced to a matter of personal choice and preference.

Nor is this mere advertising hype. For all our institutions are struggling with the consequences of what happens when you reduce wisdom to knowledge, and truth is displaced by information. Many of our universities are abandoning traditional things like the search for wisdom and truth, and becoming mere purveyors of knowledge and information. When trendy western academics say that we all have our own truth, it might sound like a kind of democracy of knowledge and behaviour, but the reality is that it is serious bad news for most of the world's people. It's like picking a slice of Christmas pudding – if you don't like the flavours you get in one piece, you simply choose another one. But if truth and wisdom are reduced to personal preferences, then there is no justice, there is no right and wrong, the Holocaust was not evil after all – and the unspoken hopes and aspirations that we all have for a better world have no chance of coming to pass. In a world where nothing is true, because everything is true, violence and exploitation tend to thrive, and violence becomes just one lifestyle choice among others.

This is why being a Christian today is both easier than it has ever been, and more difficult. On the one hand people are genuinely searching for the meaning of life, but on the other they are being sold a philosophy which says that the very thing they are looking for doesn't exist, and at best there are only personal opinions and prejudices. To be effective witnesses for Christ in this context, we need to do some radical rethinking of what it means to be a follower of Jesus Christ. No longer are we being called to put forward rational arguments for our faith. On the contrary, we are being called to take the far more risky course of allowing our own following, and the quality of life and relationships that produces – our spirituality – and say to the world: this is what God's kingdom might be like. If this appeals to you, then join us on the journey as we seek to follow Christ.

Bible Reading No. 3: Making new patterns for our community – The Magnificat (Luke 1)

What are we bringing to birth as we approach the new Millennium? How will it be crafted? What colours and styles will be used as this new area is brought to life? What kind of Church are we going to hand on to the next generation?

Bringing to birth is a metaphor we need to explore and use in our evangelism at this point in time: looking to the future as well as to the past. Motherhood may be a most appropriate metaphor for us to use as we theologically tease out what we are called to do and be as we begin to create afresh, sharing in God's creativity, for the new century. Since incarnation is at the heart of Christian faith, what more appropriate a place to look than to the experience of Mary?

One of the things that is prominent throughout her story is the affirmation that God gives to women as physical beings. Down through the centuries, men have been scared of women's reproductive capacities, and as a consequence women have often been ashamed or embarrassed about their own natural processes of fertility. Of course, this is completely contrary to the clear teaching of Scripture, which affirms at creation that we are made in God's image, male and female – and that includes especially our physical selves.

Increasing numbers of women today are rediscovering the spiritual power of their physical cycles, and using what is natural as an entry point for what is spiritual – or, rather, are insisting there is no authentic Christian distinction to be drawn between the physical and the spiritual. And herein lies one of the most distinctive contributions of motherhood to the re-emerging Christian spirituality. For a mother, the image of birth is a natural one to apply to Christian growth and development. But men, on the other hand, seem to be happier with using images of death as the starting point for their understanding of spirituality. Starting from death, we inevitably reflect on final conclusions, what we have done and what we haven't done, who is guilty for what and in what measure, how we will be judged, and so on. As a result, we can often be judgemental of one another.

But starting from birth opens up a different set of images – and our spirituality becomes not focused on guilt and mess and judgement, but instead we can look to the possibilities, move forward hand in hand with God as little children ourselves on the journey, knowing that before us lies growth and discovery and exploration, and renewal of life. Starting from birth, we encourage one another, support one another, and hold out that generous spirit that we saw to be one of the central values of God's kingdom.

If you doubt whether that is what has happened, then just reflect on how uneasy even some Christians can be with the story of the first advent, and are not satisfied until somehow we have taken the great facts of the incarnation and turned them into the cross and the atonement. It's as if we don't know how to handle Christmas, except by rushing as fast as we can to turn it into Easter. We have done our mission great harm by focusing only on one male set of images of the life of discipleship. Jesus himself never instilled a sense of guilt and failure in the people he met, but always held out the possibility of a new start, further stages on the journey, personal renewal, and fresh empowerment to be the best people we can possibly be – because we are made in God's image.

Can men ever be part of this vision of God's way of doing things? Of course, but it will be a challenging and costly thing. This is camels and eyes of needles stuff! We'll have to let go of much of the image of maleness that our culture has placed upon us. The idea that we can be self-sufficient, that we ourselves can somehow stand in the place of God. It's an offence before God when men in the church sometimes really believe they – and not women – are in the place of God. Worse than that, it's idolatry – breaking the very first commandment.

We'll need to give up the idea that spirituality is an achievement, for which there are rewards and punishments, take more seriously what Scripture says about none of us being able to do anything to save ourselves, and explore instead what it would mean for spirituality to become a journey, in which we walk alongside our children and our partners, exploring the riches that are to be found in God and through human relationships. There is a story about Abraham Lincoln. He was at a slave auction and was appalled by the sights and sounds of buying and selling human beings. His heart was especially drawn to a young woman on the block whose story seemed to be told in her eyes. She looked with hatred and contempt on all around her. She had been used and abused all her life, and this for her was just one more cruel humiliation.

The bidding began, and Lincoln offered a bid. Other amounts were bid, and he offered more – until he won. He paid the money to the auctioneer, took possession of the title deeds to this young woman, who stared at him with a vicious contempt. She asked him what he was going to do with her next. He replied 'I'm going to set you free.' 'Free for what?' she said. 'Just free – completely free,' he replied. 'Free to do whatever I want to do?' she asked. 'Yes – free to do whatever you want to do.' 'Free to say whatever I want to say?' 'Yes, free to say whatever you want to say.' 'Free to go wherever I want to go?' she added with scepticism. 'Yes, you are free to go anywhere you want to go.' 'Then I'm going with you,' she said with a smile. God's ways of doing things are what will set us all free!

John and Olive Drane *regularly work together seeking to relate the gospel to contemporary culture. Olive ministers through clowning and the arts. John is Professor of Practical Theology at the University of Aberdeen and is also a Minister of the Baptist Church of Scotland. Previously he was Director of the Centre of Christianity and Contemporary Society at the University of Stirling.*

Prophetic Evangelism – Glory and Gift

The Most Revd George Carey,
Archbishop of Canterbury

The Decade of Evangelism was initiated in 1988 at the Lambeth Conference when the assembled bishops called on the Anglican Communion to move from a culture of 'maintenance to mission'. In these remaining months of the twentieth Decade of Evangelism we are in a better position to assess the success and failure of what we set out to do. This will help us considerably as we prepare for the challenges of the twenty-first Decade but, in my view, it would be very wrong simply to see this as a 'nuts and bolts' exercise in determining what has worked in the past and what we ought to do in the future. For the Church is not a group of department stores simply concerned with numbers, products and customers. Whatever people may think about an Archbishops' Council we are not trying to please a Board of Directors or even those who might be 'shareholders'. Our task and our burden as a church is to be faithful to a God who is always in mission; an evangelizing God whose desire is to reveal himself to all.

Therefore, long before I talk about the impact of the Decade of Evangelism I want to talk about God and his mission.

I begin by quoting, incredibly enough, some words from a General Synod debate. This is not to put you to sleep but to wake you up! Let us recall for a moment, the words of a former Archdeacon of Canterbury, Bernard Pawley, speaking in Synod as long ago as 1979:

> The long-suffering clergy do not wish to be told again and again to reinterpret the gospel or make it relevant; they want help in doing it and want to hear what the gospel sounds like and looks like when it has been so treated. There is therefore here a poverty of inspiration which I find a little alarming. It seems to me at this point the whole enterprise betrays its lack of inspiration and needs to be reoriented in one particular classical direction, that of prophecy. If you are going to indulge in evangelism, you have got to have

prophets, who to my mind are singularly lacking. If you want to do evangelism, first catch your prophet.

First catch your prophet. And the most fundamental thing I notice about the prophet is his passion for God's holiness, for God's justice, for God's world and for God's Church. To read any of the Prophetic works of the Old Testament is to enter a world of intimacy with God who calls forth love, anger, indignation and suffering. The message is holistic; there is no separation of holiness from social justice or of worship from compassion for the weak. Mission and evangelism hang together.

But I also notice *glory* there. I mean by this God's glory. The glory that is fundamental to the sharing of faith in every time and place. So Isaiah in a remarkable passage about judgement suddenly speaks of God's glory:

> They lift up their voices, they sing for joy:
> Over the majesty of the Lord they shout from the west.
> Therefore in the east give glory to the Lord:
> In the coastlands of the sea, to the name of the Lord,
>   the God of Israel.
> From the ends of the earth we hear songs of praise,
> Of glory to the Righteous One (Isaiah 24.14-16)

And such a focus on glory – *doxa* – is a reminder that the Church's worship and ministry must be directed towards what, theologically, we call doxology. Mission and evangelism are rooted in God's glory and issue in praise and thanksgiving and joyful obedience. It is not surprising that churches with a real enthusiasm for evangelism and a longing for growth are those with doxology at the centre of their life. In the words of the Te Deum: 'We praise you, O God, we acknowledge you to be the Lord.' Praise turns our attention away from selfish interests to the 'raison d'être' of faith in the God of salvation.

Therefore, if the 'glory' of God is the *direction* of all mission and evangelism, then mission and evangelism are *gift* from a God who delights in giving his children the best. We have been reminded through the work of the Turnbull Commission that central to all Christian life is a theology of 'gracious gift'. What is meant by this is that all we do is rooted in God's gift of himself in Christ and the Spirit's gift in all Christian work. There is therefore no room for human boasting about human achievement or our own natural gifts; all come from the Giver.

This observation kills at once the Pelagian temptation in evangelism to make of the Christian life an exhausting world of works, of breathless

21

human activity, resulting in a burden of guilt on already overloaded parish priests and parishes. Recognizing mission and evangelism as a gift reminds us that we have nothing to offer of ourselves but only what we have been given – what we have shared and what we have enjoyed. 'O taste and see how good the Lord is!' is the motive for evangelism; the humble invitation of a receiver who becomes a sharer.

And with that brief introduction of 'glory and gift' as being central to mission I want to explore further my earlier contention that 'prophetic evangelism' has something to say to our task and to our generation.

One of the recommendations concerning mission in the report from the Lambeth conference 1998 – 'Called to Live and Proclaim the Good News' – was that 'We must pay increasing attention to culture and mission.' So, to the question: What is the missionary challenge to Anglicans in the next Millennium? The answer is: 'We must pay increasing attention to culture and mission.'

But how? My response is the attention we pay must be prophetic attention. The importance of this in the developing world has been explored quite thoroughly. Prophecy is about the redemption and transformation of culture. In those countries where injustice from governments both at home and abroad blights people's lives, the call for transformation has featured strongly in the growing volume of the prophetic cries for justice. Nor do I need to remind you of the books that have been written on these subjects, beginning with the liberation theologians of Central and South America. Their theology has given those of us in the developed world a number of useful and valuable insights, but I think many people find it difficult to see how the prophetic prescriptions of such theologians can work in this country today. How do we make our prophetic witness in the Church of England today?

Our culture seems to be one in which it is claimed Christianity is dying a natural death; literally of 'old age'. Life is not as dramatic in Britain as in Latin America or Central Africa so, perhaps, it doesn't require a Christian revelation to interpret it. We can certainly be grateful to Christianity for all it has given the country – but its moment has gone. We no longer need its structures, liturgy or life. We no longer feel the need for peace, security or hope in God. We get them from other sources: our wealth, our pleasures, our democracy. Sure, Christian evangelization works in Africa – but not here. It's no longer necessary in the affluent, self-assured first world. So the argument goes.

But it is precisely *because* we are in a society with something of an allergy to religion (even to serious thought!) that mission is crucial. A different type of mission it must be, but it is essentially the same task being performed so inspiringly in other parts of the world. The Old Testament should give us an idea of what is required. Those who witnessed to Israel before and after the Exile, were in the same business. But they had different messages, because their societies were different.

Often, liberation theologians have taken their inspiration from the prophets writing to a captive people after the Exile, with their themes of the hope of the restoration of Israel, the hope of a Messiah, the hope that one day the Israelites would be restored to favour in the eyes of their Lord and find justice. We, on the other hand, must take our inspiration from those, like Amos or Hosea, who spoke out before the calamities. These prophets were 'on a mission from God' to change the society they lived in, and the hearts and minds of its people whose reliance on prosperity for peace and security whilst denying the injustices of their society demanded such a mission from them.

So if we are to bring people to God, we need a distinctive prophetic witness which engages with our particular culture, just as Amos or Ezekiel engaged with theirs. What is more, prophets are rather like parents. They bring a mixture of inspiration and criticism. So too, there is no doubt that we need inspiration and indeed, a bit of self-searching criticism in this country at present. There are some hard things that need to be acknowledged by a prophetic mission. We must be honest about the kind of society we seek to serve at the turn of the century – a society which includes ourselves.

We are a society oppressed, in the main, not by lack, but by surfeit, not by strife, but by ease. Of course there is real poverty in our midst, but most people have benefited enormously from the rises in real incomes over the past few decades. We have gone from 'You've never had it so good' to 'You never had it too bad'. Few of us remain who can remember the last World War when we were literally on our beam-ends. And we have paid a price for such comfort and ease. We are in a situation where the things of ultimate importance are invisible, obscured by the things of transitory glamour. The 'love that abides forever' cannot easily endure in such a culture. The Church says that now, and part of its mission will be to keep on saying it.

And we must be honest that when we do mission, when we try to witness to the God who has called us, we are criticizing such a society. The public we seek to evangelize are not stupid. They know that very often, the gospel being preached to them is an implicit criticism of their way of life. They are not going to like it. But particularly they will not like it if we try and disguise that fact. Or if we try to hide the radical implications of following this Lord. If all we say is: yes it's obvious you lead a wonderful life with your two lovely children, your two holidays a year, your two cars, two televisions, two videos, two microwaves, two heated towel rails . . . but – you also need God in your life. That's all that's missing.

And too often, we make out that that is the case: that people are substantially all right – and that they just need to come to know Jesus as well. That, as we have to admit, is all a little too cosy and cheap. As Dietrich Bonhoeffer reminded the Church of his day, cheap grace sells the gospel short. It is merely an 'add on' faith. A true, prophetic mission will not be that easy to swallow.

Furthermore, we must be honest with ourselves about the receptivity of our audience. They are not, as we might be tempted to believe, a group of little lost lambs who are conscious that they would be happy if only they could find a shepherd. To believe that there is a *real* spiritual hunger is one thing – which some question – but then to suggest that there is a simple answer to it in Christianity is another. As the Israelites were described to Ezekiel, so we may see the people, including church people, to whom we witness. 'They are stubborn and obstinate.' We cannot deny the wilfulness and obstinacy of human nature. Our own capacity for self-deception, pride and self-gratification is limitless. We know it; we all know it.

Which brings me on to the final 'challenge of a prophetic mission'. If we are to throw a few stones, we must be wary that our house isn't made of glass. We must be self-critical as well. Prophecy, being about redemption and transformation, has to apply to the Church of England. We may criticize our culture for being self-interested, but so often we are seen as wanting to hang on to what we have, like the wealthy young man who turned away from Jesus with a heavy heart caught between the hunger to serve God and the cost it entails. The maintenance versus mission debate is old hat now, of course, and we realize we must strike a balance between the two duties. We realize that part of maintenance is presence, and that presence is part of mission. But we must guard constantly against complacency – and self-preservation – and be prepared to sacrifice the old and the comfortable in order to advance the gospel. That, indeed, is a long-established duty of Christians.

How then do we get inside the modern human condition? How does the gospel engage intellectually with modern, thinking people? Immanuel

Kant described the three major questions confronting every thinking person as: 'What can we know? What ought we to do? What can we hope for?'

And these questions about 'meaning', about 'morality' and about 'destiny' are fundamental to us all. But they can't be reduced to the mantra: 'Come along to church and all will be explained.' Authentic Christianity surely includes church going but it is far richer than this. It is a way of life. It is the joyful adventure of entering into the mission of God. It is the risk-filled challenge to take up our cross and follow Christ.

So then, what can we do? How may we be once again relevant to our culture and society?

And the only authentic answer we can give is by being 'incarnational'. The example is Christ himself. He did not withdraw from life; he lived fully within it and scandalized the religious and the secular establishments of his day. His mission was a seamless robe of 'mission' and 'evangelism'. Social care rubbed shoulders naturally with his call for people to follow him; his anger at hypocrisy was all of a piece with his compassion for lepers and the very poor. His teaching about the kingdom was in tune with his condemnation of social evil.

David Bosch, in many ways the founder of modern missiological thinking, says this:

> It belongs to our missionary mandate to ask questions about the use of power in our societies, to unmask those that destroy life, to show concern for the victims of society while at the same time calling to repentance those who have turned them into victims, and to articulate God's active wrath against all that distorts and diminishes human beings and all that exploits, squanders and disfigures the world.

This is a prophetic mission. It is a mission we must perform, in the midst of our dis-eased culture, with a vision of how things might be.

And this brings me to my reflections on the Decade of Evangelism. No one planned that the Decade would also include our decision to settle the matter of the ordination of women to the priesthood, with its inevitable consequences for time and money. Similarly, no one foresaw that at the same time we would have on our hands a financial crisis of mega proportions as the Church Commissioners assets declined by 20 per cent. But these distractions have not halted our determination to make mission and evangelism central to all we stand for. Through the work of the Board of Mission – whose energy and vision I salute; through initiatives like Alpha,

Emmaus, and Springboard; through teachers and theologians such as Robert Warren, we are beginning to affect the culture of the Church of England. Decline is no longer seen as the inevitable destination of the Church although it is still the tired, old song of some of our critics. They still ignore the fact that giving continues to rise in our parishes and that ordination figures are up for the fourth year running. There is a rising confidence and optimism in our church which continues to thrill me.

And prophetic mission has never been lacking in the way Anglicans have seen mission and evangelism. Our ministry has always been incarnational at its best. Think of the parish ministry and its structures. Consider those parishes – and they are more numerous than some are prepared to admit – where the daily round of worship, service, study and pastoral care is all about mission. The late and great Peter Green of Salford has much to teach us. He once said: 'My object is first of all to gather a congregation, large, converted, instructed and missionary-hearted and then to set it to work. First, forge, temper and sharpen your sword; and then wield it.' And there are still many parishes like that.

But extending our gaze beyond the parishes of our land we should note our commitment to schools, and our work in prisons, hospitals and the armed forces as part, also, of our incarnational and prophetic approach to ministry. The astonishing work of the Church Urban Fund arose from the protest expressed in *Faith in the City* that we cannot tolerate the exploitation of the poor in the urban environment. I think too of our passion for the world's poor and the removal of the chains around Africa through Jubilee 2000, so wonderfully articulated by Lambeth '98 and at that service at St Paul's last Sunday. Admittedly, all this taken together as mission – which I truly believe it is – may require a sharper focus. But my point is that we are engaging with our culture and the Church is appreciated for so doing.

You see, when all is said and done, the Church's concern is not the Church but the kingdom of God. 'The kingdom of God' declared Jürgen Moltmann 'isn't there for the sake of the Church. The Church is there for the sake of the kingdom.' We must never forget it. The Church's mandate from our Lord is to proclaim the gospel of God's kingdom to all human beings. In this way, evangelization and prophetic mission complement and enrich each other. Consequently, the health of our churches must be assessed according to the degree they look away from their own interests into God's concerns and those of the world around.

But lest I am accused of seeing only a vague picture from a distance, and leaving it unrelated to this conference and the work going on in our dioceses, let me say something of what has been happening in my own

Diocese of Canterbury in response to the Decade, as I believe this has a great deal to teach us in relation to that wider picture.

In 1995 the Bishop of Maidstone described to the Diocesan Synod some of the factors that are important for churches to grow. He produced this from a careful study of 16 parishes where growth was happening. The churches were different in churchmanship, social background and included rural and urban churches. He noted six things:

1. In each case the *leadership* of the church longed for growth to happen.

2. Each church was eager to *build bridges into the community*. A parish, not a congregational mentality, is important.

3. *Teaching* was dominant in each of the churches because it was felt vital to help people grow in their faith.

4. There was an emphasis on *excellence and thoroughness*.

5. In each case the *congregation* was involved in decision making.

6. There was a *range of different liturgies* to meet different needs and so create new congregations.

But I want to add to his list a seventh item which was also common to the churches referred to, and has arisen time and again in my own experience, over the years. For *excellence in worship* is also a key to growth. Of course, the word 'excellence' does not have to mean the same in each place. It does, however, convey the idea of 'thoroughness' in preparation; of being in touch with the needs of the community the church seeks to serve, as well as reflecting the traditions of our church; and of worship where the standards of music are high and where participation is also emphasized. Dull, complicated and poorly led worship coupled with indifferent teaching are factors that lead to decline.

Of course, I doubt whether these seven points are particularly new and I'm sure there are many other places throughout the country where similar things have been identified. What interests me is that this set of characteristics brings together mission and evangelism and helps to create healthy churches.

I think of one such church in part of a very needy area of Ramsgate. There the church is actively engaged in serving the community through a range of activities including using one of the estate's empty shops to meet social needs. A young priest is there reaching out in a way that may legitimately be called prophetic – and the church is seeing steady growth.

In another parish growth has been nurtured through a consistent and persistent visiting programme. The building of caring relationships has drawn people into the worshipping community.

In another parish there is a determined attempt to focus on baptism and to draw the very young in to the fellowship. How sad that so few churches see baptism as a powerful evangelistic and missionary tool.

Of course not everything we try works. There are failures and we must learn from these. Many of the churches in the Canterbury Diocese struggle with reaching older children and young people. For many the Sunday school is on its last legs if it hasn't already disappeared. That is why in some parishes, and I can think of one very exciting example, the running of a mid-week after school club has become the model to emulate.

It is also why the diocese has a children's missioner who works with children as well as having a children's officer to help train leaders in children's work.

And I welcome too the increasing number of full-time youth officers being employed by churches to stimulate work among the young. I was told during my visit to the Oxford Diocese that in Buckinghamshire the Church now has more youth workers than the statutory authorities.

All of this and many other examples throughout the country tell me that we are seeing a real mission engagement to our culture.

But let us not see the end of this decade as a winding down. A cutting back of those actively involved in mission. Rather let us see this as the foundation upon which we continue to build. Thus, as we come to the end of the Decade of Evangelism we must warn dioceses not to heave a sigh of relief and say: 'Now it is business as usual. Back to the safe and welcome activity of keeping the Church going.' But mission and evangelism are truly 'business as usual' because that is what the Church is for; to proclaim afresh the glory of God and the gift of Jesus Christ. Nothing less will do.

The Church, as I have said on countless occasions, is one generation away from extinction. And our generation is being called to hand on our torch of faith to the generations of the third Millennium. It will require all our vigour, all our energy, all our faith and enthusiasm. And it is God's prophetic mission we share. It is a concern and a commitment that, I am sure, the new Archbishops' Council will take to heart as must each bishop and every diocese.

Some years ago I recall going to St Paul's Church, Deptford when David Diamond was vicar. What wonderful work continues there to this day! We sang in that extraordinary Commemorative Mass the modern hymn 'Our God Reigns'. But the printer made two terrible mistakes in the hymn. In verse 2 the printer had printed: 'Our Gold reigns' which in that part of London was a howler of great proportions. In verse 3 we ended up singing: 'Our God resigns' which also made the south London congregation very amused. But resigning is not his habit. It is his world we are serving; it is his work we are doing; it is in his power that our mission finds its strength – and because he reigns, we take heart.

Evangelism
in a Post-Religious Society

Paul Vallely

At a party recently I met someone who seemed to personify the problems that the Church has in speaking to the modern world in Britain today. Cathy is a thoughtful, caring, intelligent mother with two children. The wife of a senior ICI manager she is active at the school of one child, and in the playgroup of the other. She's an activist in the local community and in environmental action groups, the kind of woman you might describe as a pillar of the modern community.

She's 40 and was brought up in a mainstream denomination but she has drifted away. And yet drifted is not quite the right word, for it suggests a lack of effort and application, which is not missing in her life.

I told her I wrote about religion and she volunteered directly: 'Oh! I'm really interested in religion, though, of course, I don't go to church now.' The 'of course' was revealing; for it shows that in Cathy's circles it was the norm not to be an active churchgoer.

When had she last been to church? 'Oh, I went to Midnight Mass at Christmas to keep my Mum happy. But it made me realize that the Church has nothing to say these days.' It was, she said, a lot of mumbo jumbo, all those meaningless words, all done by rote, the vestments and ritual from another era, dominated by men who were out of touch with the reality of modern life and the problems people lived with. She needed spirituality, and all the Church offered was stale and arid repetition. (I noticed that she talked always about 'the Church'. There was no mention of Christ or of Jesus, just 'the Church' – a faceless, distant, male organization that is totally out of touch with her life and what's important in it.)

But she described herself as a 'very spiritual person'. She has begun to read New Age philosophies – the American writer Carolyn Myss and books like *The Celestine Prophecy*. This was the stuff that really excited her. 'Carolyn Myss is fantastic; you must read her. I read her books and then re-read them and I think I'm really starting to understand her and get to grips with the ideas.'

As we spoke it became clear that there was nothing idle about her interest. She is very serious about her quest. She even asked her husband to read the books so they could discuss them. Later I asked him about it all. He shrugged. He had 'no real interest in any of that kind of stuff' he said, but he had read it to please her and found 'it was actually quite interesting'. There was, he said, definitely something in it.

Some effective New Age evangelism had gone on here – though Cathy would not dream of using the word. Terms like 'evangelism' and 'mission' have something dead about them to her – they are words, people in this hall would do well to bear in mind, which throw up an insurmountable barrier of suspicion to most people in the secular world. They feel preyed upon by them.

For Cathy there is something positive about her decision to abandon the Church and look elsewhere. It is not apathy, or what the Pope calls indifferentism. She is making considerable effort to seek out something that 'works for her'. It is not just a passive thing. She was prepared to 'read the books and then re-read them' where she was prepared to make no effort any longer with the Nicene creed and its opaque formulations which reflect the preoccupations of obscure fourth-century Greek philosophy. She saw no advantage in seeking out Jesus behind the formulae, the hierarchy, the doctrine and dogma of virgin birth and immaculate conception. These are, to people like her, seen as obstacles rather than aids to spiritual development. But she *would* 'read and re-read' some Californian New Age guru whose use of jargon was probably no less than that of the theologians of Nicea, but whose very jargon with its psycho-talk of self-fulfilment somehow spoke more directly to her. 'I think I'm really starting to understand her and get to grips with the ideas,' she said.

And then she went on: 'We're the transitional generation. The Church and its language does nothing for me. *It's up to us to hand something different on to our children.*' What she was searching for was some realistic and meaningful way of expressing a spirituality – and using it to enhance her life and her contribution to the community and common good – and then passing those values on to her children. And the Church had no place in that for her.

Over the past six months I have met many women like Cathy. The brief for my column in *The Independent* each Saturday is to look at what people in present-day Britain believe in. It's called 'Spirit of the Age' and it encompasses everything from taking part in a service of Orthodox Judaism to some of the wilder New Age vagaries. If it is a belief which affects the way people live their lives then it is fair game. It has been, you might say, a mind-broadening experience.

What I want to do this morning is *not* to tell you how you should be evangelizing contemporary society. But, instead, to draw on some of that wider range of experience, with mainstream communities from all the major faiths, as well as the exotic extrusions of the New Age, to try to describe the world in which you have set yourselves the task of evangelism – and to try to draw from those experiences some questions about what it is people are looking for – which they are not finding in the Church – by which I mean the mainstream indigenous British denominations. I will offer four lessons which the Churches might draw.

By now we all know about the size of the problem. The statistics are familiar. For two centuries the Church has been in apparent decline. Membership of Protestant churches has fallen from 22 per cent of British adults in 1900 to 6 per cent today.[1] Active membership of religious organizations fell from 9.8 million to 8.3 million people between 1970 and 1995.[2] Yet, as we also know, the statistics also show that – if religion is in decline – belief is not. And if the massive and authoritative 1990 European Values Survey shows that though most people now don't expect answers from the Church, the number who regularly feel the need for prayer, meditation or contemplation was 53 per cent – 3 per cent *up* on a decade earlier. In that intervening ten years the percentage of the population which emerges as avowedly atheist went up from 4 per cent to only 4.4 per cent.[3]

The controversial creation theologian Matthew Fox sees that positively. Post-Sixties men and women, he says, are not interested in religion but in spirituality. Yet sociologists of religion have suggested that modern belief outside the Church manifests itself in something rather odd. There is some evidence that those who say they do not go to church, but say they are religious and pray quite often, have moved much closer to what would normally be called superstition.[4] Their beliefs, says Grace Davie, 'are of an increasingly individualized and unorthodox nature'.[5] And she wrote that before the Glenn Hoddle saga.

It is easy to mock the New Age – and much of it is worthy of mockery. After I met Cathy I went out and bought *The Celestine Prophecy*. I cannot say I recommend it, except perhaps as a way of getting the measure of what you are up against. It is written in the style of a bad airport thriller, larded with a mixture of modern world-weary cynicism and superstitious gullibility. Woven into the detective story is the search for a lost Peruvian manuscript which contains the Nine Insights that will move the earth towards a completely spiritual culture. The book, like so much New Age material, is a mixture of self-evident platitudes and implausible science fiction, with touches borrowed from religions of both East and West, all wrapped up in a Gnostic sense (common enough in most religious traditions at some point) that there are arcane secrets which can be handed down from some other place to special people – of whom you can be one if only you will cooperate!

But, whether or not this is egregious nonsense, the key question remains – what do so many people get out of this stuff. To find out I went to talk to an extraterrestrial entity, called Omar. It was not, I have to say, terribly successful. I tried to go with an open mind. After all, you would be fairly dismissive of Buddhism if you merely described it as the teachings of a man who sat in a cave and did nothing. Or Islam as based on a book dictated to a camel-trader by an angel in a dream. Or Christianity if it was reduced to the description of those who believe that God was born in a stable, was killed and then rose from the dead. So perhaps Omar the extraterrestrial might also have some beneficial impact upon the lives of believers and on the rest of the world.

So, I took myself off to an alternative 'healing centre' in Brighton, full of crystals, aromatic oils and weird American videos, and decided to discount the fact that he was an extraterrestrial and see what fruits he bore. When I had rung up to make an appointment with the woman through whom Omar communicates with the world, her minder Clive sounded rather fierce. Omar was not a doctor, he said, he would not tell me about, my health or my job or my love life. Just my spiritual growth. 'Right,' I said. And I should come along with a list of spiritual questions, said Clive, because Omar didn't speak unprompted – he only answered questions. 'Right,' I said.

I jotted a few questions down on the train on the way there. You know the sort of thing: How do I achieve inner peace? Should we strive for knowledge or detachment? Why is there suffering in the world? What is evil? What happens at the end of this life? What must I do to gain eternal life? And so forth.

This, however, was not what Omar wanted. I arrived at the Brighton healing centre to be ushered upstairs past a rickety wooden gate and into the presence of the medium. She was a large woman, in a gigantic floral skirt, who sat immobile on a bed surrounded by cushions. In one hand she held a green glass globe which she held as she closed her eyes and started to twitch her arms. Her high-pitched voice became suddenly husky with extraterrestrial presence and she announced the arrival of the entity from the other world with the words: 'Omar ready.'

For a resident of an outer dimension, Omar had an admirable grasp of colloquial English, especially of the Californian variety. He advised me to get in contact with my Higher Self. And when I asked what were its requirements he told me that there were no requirements – 'only hope or desire'. I did not need communion with others to do this, Omar said, only 'a focus on inner self'.

I was beginning to get the picture. This seemed familiar New Age territory. The enlightenment and harmony being ushered in by the Age of Aquarius seems singularly focused on desire rather than the spirit of discipline required by the established religions. Monism, relativism and individual autonomy is apparently where we are all heading in our quest for greater knowledge and a new consciousness.

Would the Higher Self continue after death? But when I asked that, Omar began to go ungrammatical and even more impenetrable. 'I don't quite follow,' I said, 'are you saying there is life after death, or not?'

The large lady twitched her am-dram shudder once more. She opened her eyes. 'He has broken the connection,' she said in her ordinary voice. 'He did not like the questions. They are too outside, not from inside. Call for Clive. These are not the kind of questions people usually ask.'

So what kind of questions did people usually ask, I wondered. She muttered, but nothing coherent. Back came Clive, a burly balding chap with wispy hair at the sides and straggly sideburns. They sent me from the room and went into a holy huddle. When they called me back it was to tell me that I was not spiritual enough for channelling. It was too advanced for me. Perhaps I should try Tarot readings, which would be £20.

I told this story to Martin Palmer, the director of ICOREC, a Christian who has made a study of the New Age, and suggested it might all have been a fraud. Of course it was, he said, and added that in his experience four-fifths of all New Age practitioners were charlatans.

And yet you have to take this stuff seriously, simply because there is so much of it around. Even in the Seventies, when John Hinnells's *Handbook of Living Religions* was first published, the rise in what was then called 'psychic' and 'magical' new religions was estimated at 104 times higher than the popularity of more mainstream 'new' religions like Mormonism. In the two decades since then the New Age movement has grown exponentially to become a significant feature of the Western world's spiritual life. Today there are 16,000 New Religious Movements in Britain alone, according to Eileen Barker at INFORM. And as much as 25 per cent of the adult population are said to have explored New Age ideas in some way. At the last

United Nations Conference on Freedom of Religion and Belief, under the beady eye of its High Commissioner on Human Rights, Mary Robinson, equal status was given alongside established religions to what it called 'the Holistic and New Age movement'.

Why is this? Anxieties always rise as civilizations decline, said Paul Tillich. Today – when European domination of the world is over, America's is peaking and economic power is shifting to the Pacific Rim – there can be little doubt that a sense of dejection is evident in many sections of Western society. The values of the Enlightenment are under threat. The science, capitalism, modernity which brought us antibiotics, foreign holidays and consumer gadgets have also brought us nuclear weapons, the gas chamber, pollution and toxic waste. We still have widescale unemployment, a rise in casualization and part-time work – and the growth of the contract culture. Combine this with the degradation of public services and rising crime levels and the result is that high degrees of risk and uncertainty have become routine. Stress is reaching unprecedented levels in our society. There is a general intuition of a society, fragmenting under economic pressures and the anti-social philosophies of the market. With globalization the process is writ large and seems even more out of control.

It is a world of Social Darwinism. From a culture of contentment we have moved to a culture of resentment: those in work, work too hard, and yet are insecure; those who are without a job find themselves increasingly sentenced to long-term unemployment and dismissal as the 'underclass'. For all the material wealth – the two cars, two holidays, two videos world the archbishop spoke of yesterday – there is a sense of the world being increasingly out of control. Of the death of a sense of the common good. Of a generation growing up without spiritual values. No wonder people speak of pre-millennial tension.

Much of the population retreat into the materialist laager which has scientific rationalism at one end and hedonistic pleasure-seeking at the other. But increasing numbers seek solace or try to gain some sense of control in a different level of reality. The rationalists have turned to secular forms of solidarity with single issue groups like Oxfam or Amnesty, or on the environment, animal rights, or Third World Debt. Those whose seeking is more overtly spiritual, turn to the attractions of the New Age.

There is one other thing. At the start of our century few people had many dealings with strangers. Our grandparents conducted most of their relationships with other people face to face. The change since their time would be hard for them to imagine. Today we are connected to others in a different way. Our telephone can link us with almost a billion people throughout the world. The Internet gives us the ability to shift vast amounts of information across thousands of miles in just seconds. But if our interconnectedness is greater it is also more flimsy. For these new technologies simultaneously seem to dilute our sense of obligation to those we encounter. The information technology revolution has been like the car – which made travel easier but developed the separateness of the suburb. Television and the computer have offered the illusion of contact with far-off worlds whilst keeping them psychologically distant. All of which enables us to hide behind anonymity and, as one commentator has put it, to 'surround ourselves with more fleeting transactions that demand less in terms of understanding and intimacy.'[6] Today we belong to a very different world to the one predicted in the middle of the twentieth century by Teilhard de Chardin who imagined that technological change would interlock with human destinies to produce a spiritual progress which would end in the unity of everything with God.

The New Age speaks to this contradiction at the heart of modern life. Science is a blessing – but also a curse. Capitalism creates wealth – but also inequality. Modern individualism is a benefit – and also a burden. The shrinking of our sense of connectedness is both a release – and a limitation. New Agers want to have it both ways in all these paradoxes. They want simultaneously to embrace the comforts of materialism – to find something beyond them. To them the Church has no part to play here for it is seen as part of the contradiction of modernity. Modern people want new ways out. Or more exactly they want to redefine the problem so that the old issues – and ways of dealing with them – seem irrelevant.

So what are the needs which people are identifying within themselves and which the Church is, in their eyes, failing to meet? Remember, I am not here endorsing the demands of the New Agers, only identifying certain characteristics which the Church has to grapple with if it is not to decline into insignificance.

What can we tease out of what I have said so far – of the experience of Cathy – as a response to the socio-economic circumstance of the age. I identify four things:

First, people today start with themselves. The message from California is about personal development and personal fulfilment. Even where those like Cathy are looking outside themselves – at their relationship with a sense of Other or of others – they begin with themselves. They do not start with another person, a book, a revelation, a creed, a dogma or an institution. All of that kind of thing is perceived as alienating them from their direct experience.

If this sounds in profound contrast to Christian notions of service and self-emptying it is perhaps worth thinking of the work of Latin America's liberation theologians who began, not with the Bible, but with the experience of the poor. The poor, taught Paolo Freire, do not lack intelligence but only education and even literacy. They are aware of the injustices of life around them but lack a wider perspective which enables them to see the relationship between the different component parts. Give them that and you give them the power they need to change things. Theology 'rises only at sundown' said Gustavo Gutierrez.[7] It can come only out of faith which comes out of life. Therefore theology can only be a 'second act' which follows the 'first act' of finding faith in Christ's commitment to the poor. The first book is life; the second book is the Bible, he said. 'Theology is an understanding of the faith'[8] and that understanding must be found by the poor themselves. If expert guidance is needed to provide support from scripture or the tradition of the Church it should come from theologians who live and work amongst the poor, as Christ did. There are clear parallels and lessons for responding to the hunger of the New Agers here.

The second lesson we can draw from the testimony of the Cathys of our time, is the preference for the novel, the new, rather than the accustomed or the habitual. Even where the New Age espouses truths which are perfectly consonant with – or even drawn from Christianity – it talks a different language, a language of the time rather than of the past, a language of experience rather than theology. Yet this, too, does not seem an insurmountable obstacle.

But let me come to a third lesson, drawn this time from a visit to Sharpham College for Buddhist Studies and Contemporary Inquiry in Devon. It is run by Stephen Batchelor, a scholar in classical Tibetan, Sanskrit and Pali. Like many others in the Sixties and Seventies he was attracted to the hippy Himalayas.

Then youth had the affluence and emotional security to explore the side of the human psyche which had been neglected since the Enlightenment when the Western psyche was rent asunder into the dualism of rationalism and romanticism, with the former increasingly – as time went by – in the ascendant. By the Sixties the romantic impulse had declared that materialism, science and progress had – by jettisoning intuition – created a spiritual vacuum. They went East to recapture it – and learned hard lessons in the process.

'You people in the West,' one lama said, 'you like the mystery of it all, the magic, the talk of reincarnations, all the costumes and the rituals. It's very exotic. But these things aren't important. The real miracle of Buddhism is how a person can change, from a very empty person to a person who's full of compassion.' After ten years as a Buddhist monk in first the Tibetan and then the Zen traditions Batchelor, as he put it, 'one day realized that I was still Stephen Batchelor from Watford, and couldn't live with the split identity.'

But he has not turned to Christianity. Rather he has stripped Buddhism of its Hindu cosmology – and idea of endless rebirth and death in cycles of reincarnation. 'You don't have to accept Asian cultural norms. Buddhism is, essentially, a technique for living rather than a belief system,' he says. It is a process – a method of coming to terms with the anguish at the heart of the human condition and of detaching oneself from it. All the rituals and doctrines which the centuries have subsequently accreted to it can be done away with. He has thus formulated a Buddhism for agnostics, a religion with great appeal to the modern scientific temperament, a 'Buddhism without Beliefs'. His book of that name is a massive best-seller in the United States and now looks set to take off here.

This, then, is the third lesson I invite you to draw. That the modern temperament is more sympathetic to process than to philosophy, to integrity rather than rules, to practice rather than doctrine. What, you should ask yourselves, are the implications of that?

So to the fourth point. A couple of weeks ago I interviewed a witch, or an adept of the Wiccan religion as she preferred to style herself. Again it would have been easy to scoff. She was called Phyllis and was not just an ordinary witch but the founder and High Priestess of the Circle of Ara and the Minoan Fellowship in New York. This was the opening of her book:

> Moonlight filters in through the city skylight. The air is fragrant with the scent of flowers and the smoke of burning incense. Candles flicker and glow, bathing our bodies in golden light. Holding hands, we begin a quiet chant: 'Isis, Astarte, Diana, Hecate, Demeter, Kali . . .' Singing the names of ancient goddesses, our voices blend and rise, our bodies sway and dance, faster and faster we circle . . .

This, of course, is a load of romantic tosh. The idea that modern witchcraft lies in unbroken tradition with what its adherents like to describe as 'the old religions' has been thoroughly demolished over the past decade by scholars like Ronald Hutton who have shown that very few 'traditions' go back beyond the eighteenth century and many of these were self-conscious post-Restoration revivals after the decades of Puritanism which followed the English Civil War. Worse than that, many of the modern Wiccan rituals were invented in the 1950s by a British chap called Gerald Gardner.

Most British Pagans get cross when you say this. But Phyllis Curott, as well as being a witch, is a philosophy graduate from Brown University and earns her living as a lawyer in Manhattan specializing in anti-discrimination cases. Not a lady you would cross, for she does not need to resort to hexes or spells to deal with opponents.

Being a postmodern kind of American witch, she had the good grace to acknowledge the confectionery nature of modern witchcraft. 'Yes, this is a new spirituality,' she told me. 'Ours is a magpie religion.' Indeed. Along with Gardner's occultist inventions she mixes into her witch's cauldron hefty dollops of feminism, Jungian psychotherapy and the new eco-consciousness of our times. But such syncretism she sees as a strength rather than a weakness. 'It helps us address the imbalances of the modern world – breaking through to a non-scientific level of reality, re-emphasizing the Female Principle, and learning that what we do to the earth we do to ourselves.' Witchcraft is, she insists, a very contemporary religion. 'It is consonant with quantum physics and chaos theory – the idea that everything is bundles of vibrating interacting energy, that forms change but the energy is constant, that everything is interconnected – is both ancient and modern.'

This is significant for a number of reasons. It underscores the hunger for mystique rather than the mundane – something which Olive and John Drane touched on yesterday, and Bishop Lindsay when he feared we had 'tamed' the Eucharist. There is certainly nothing tame about Phyllis's witchy dancing.

But this modern witchcraft is also a religion of democracy, which stresses inclusion rather than hierarchy. And, it taps into the need for the feminine in the contemporary psyche, which the mainstream churches have resisted or minimized. More than that, it is not a human-centred vision of the world, which strikes a chord with the burgeoning eco-consciousness in our times – and which many accuse the Church of having curbed with a traditional insistence on putting man and woman at the centre of a universe created for their benefit and domination. And it also embraces a wide diversity of beliefs and emphases within its 'earth mother' umbrella.

This last quality is something significant throughout the New Age movement. Those outside it tend to condemn the New Age as a pick 'n' mix approach to religion – as if Judaism hadn't borrowed from Zoroastrianism, Buddhism from Hinduism, Christianity from Judaism, and Islam from both. The New Age goes one step further. It does not just tolerate diversity, it embraces it and celebrates it.

This was brought home to me when I met Dr William Bloom – a former publisher, LSE academic and special needs social worker – who now runs something called the Spiritual Freedom Network and was the man responsible for getting the New Age parity at the UN Religions conference.

'Religion is not about belief systems,' he told me. 'It's about our natural instinct to connect with beauty. It's there in us all. The old religions had tried to make out that mystical experiences were the province of a select few. But they are available for everyone.' Only in the New Age there are no rules, no conditions, no need for discipline, no requirement of consistency. Everything is equally valid. All paths can lead to spiritual fulfilment. All are welcome to join in – and those who join are not subject to the caveats of orthodoxy which are conditions of the welcome into Christianity.

The New Age does not exclude. It has no single starting point, no one set of foundation beliefs and no single teacher. Instead it has many different sources – including sub-atomic physics and theories of complexity and chaos; psychology, ecology, health and healing, feminism, tribal traditions, the mystical traditions of all the world's faiths.

'We're in a new historical period,' Bloom told me. 'Mass industrialization. The electronic and information revolutions. Mass communications. Mushrooming world population and urbanization. A global culture,' he said. 'Religion is being re-invented to suit the times. Where old religions were about hierarchy and control the New Age movement was pluralistic, diverse, democratic, networked, decentralized and post-modern. There can be no doubting the pull of that.'

You might not agree with any of this. But it is evident why it appeals to the democratic, tolerant, pluralistic temper of our times. There can, as Bloom says, be no doubting the pull of it.

There is an opposing response to all this – a backlash. It is the call of fundamentalism. It is most evident in contemporary Britain in the Muslim community, where the pressures of alienation from modern life are perhaps greater. One of my contacts returned to his native Bradford after a ten-year absence and told me: 'Before there was one group, all struggling with the tensions between two worlds. Now there are three groups: one has become very religious and introspective, another has become completely secular and pleasure-seeking, while the third drifts in the middle.' About 10 to 15 per cent have become very devout and more militant. They have turned to a purer Islam, uncontaminated by the cultural elements added by their parents, many of whom insist on preserving practices no longer followed today in Pakistan. Some even condemn arranged marriages as un-Islamic. They are vocal and uncompromising and have difficulties with their own community.

The older generation is uncertain what to do – but they sense this fundamentalism is not the way forward. Most Bradford Muslims are, rather, now much more willing to enter into dialogue with the rest of society and to discuss without striking their previous defensive or apologetic pose. In the report after the riots, the Asian member of the three-person inquiry issued a minority report in which he said the massive under-achievement of Muslim children in the city's schools was partly the community's own fault. He cited two factors. The first was a 'mosque culture' which exacerbated language difficulties by conducting its teaching entirely in Urdu and Arabic. The second was 'transcontinental marriages' – half of all Bradford Muslim marriages involve a partner from abroad, usually an uneducated rural cousin, which creates a family in which one parent is not an English speaker invariably setting back the children's education. These are bold concessions – and point the way to a new willingness by Muslims to enter into dialogue with a culture whose values are still predominantly Christian. Their own extremists respond with fundamentalism.

They are not alone. The same dynamics are at work elsewhere. Scientific rationalism has begun to throw up evangelical fundamentalist atheists like Richard Dawkins. And the search for old certainties is one response among Christians too. I have written, somewhat critically, in another of my 'Spirit of the Age' columns, of an Alpha course I attended. For it too (at least in the group I attended) took refuge in such certainties – attempting to 'prove' the existence of God with arguments from design which went out with Aquinas – or asserting the veracity of Christianity from 'historical evidence' and a whole raft of challengeable assumptions about the gospel texts. 'Facts are facts whether we choose to believe them or not,' said the rather breathless young Sloane who led my group. Christ's life fulfilled Old Testament prophesy – 'and after all he couldn't have rigged where he lived and died'. Jesus made some 'pretty wild' claims about himself – that he was the Son of God and so on. So thinking that 'Jesus was a pretty OK guy who said some good stuff' wasn't enough. He was, therefore, either God, a liar or a madman. So, she concluded, since Jesus was obviously too good to be a fraud or mad he must be God. It was all terribly sincere and well-intentioned but 'facts are not facts' when we are talking about individuals' experience of the living God. For too many people, me included, Alpha jumps deftly across the fissures of faith and crevices of doubt which give Christianity its rich complexity and reveal its depth. It does not communicate with those of 'vague faith' who want to explore the richness of God's mystery rather than to tie up God's loose ends with sequences of Scriptural quotations or neat theological formulae.

I am running out of time and I am aware that I have confined my remarks to spiritual predilections which are largely middle class. As my earlier economic analysis suggested the nation is becoming increasingly more middle class in its aspirations, even if not in the kind of economic security which was once a touchstone of the life of the British bourgeoisie. Of those who are left behind in the expansion of Middle England I have had little recent contact. And I am sure that the disenfranchised group which the free-marketeers like to call the 'under-class' present an entirely different challenge. There the hierarchy of needs puts material security often before the spiritual search – or else offers the temptation of seeking transcendence only through drugs. There, in my experience, the evangelization of the Church though insufficiently widespread is powerful and effective. I have seen enough of Christians at work in grim estates like Blackbird Leys or Easterhouse to know that the evangelical injunction of St Francis is honourably discharged – to 'preach often, and if necessary use words'.

But for the rest of the nation the challenge is different. Ours is a people which, today:

> starts with the self;

> places a premium on personal fulfilment;

> is enticed by mystique rather than mundanity, spirituality rather than theology, and prefers the new over the well-worn and habitual;

which

> has a vision that is no longer exclusively human-centred;

> seeks a spirituality that celebrates the feminine;

which

> is tolerant of diversity

and which

looks for practice not doctrine, integrity rather than rules, inclusion rather than hierarchy.

Ours is a people who do not, any longer, speak your language. Can you learn theirs? That is the challenge.

Notes

1.   S. Bruce, 'Religion in Britain at the close of the twentieth century', *Journal of Contemporary Religion*, vol. 11, no. 3 (1996), 264.

2.   According to the 1997 edition of the National Statistics Office's Social Trends. (According to one 1996 poll, 69 per cent of the population consider themselves Christians. Of those 71 per cent believed in the Resurrection.)

3.   *European Values Survey*, Jan Kerkhofs, Louvain, 1990.

4.   *Sociological Yearbook of Religion*, SCM Press, 1970.

5.   'The Individualisation of British Beliefs' in *Keeping the Faiths*, Demos Quarterly 11, 1997.

6.   Geoff Mulgan, 'Connexity: how to live in a connected world', *Resurgence Magazine*, No. 184.

7.   G. Gutierrez, A *Theology of Liberation*, Orbis Books, 1973.

8.   Gutierrez, op. cit.

Paul Vallely *is a journalist with* The Independent. *He has reported from 30 Two-Thirds World Countries and is Chairman of Traidcraft Exchange and the Catholic Institute for International Relations.*

Inner-City Evangelism

Rose Hudson-Wilkin

Confidence in the gospel

We are all familiar with the words of the Creed 'We believe.' Week after week we rattle them off our tongues but what do they mean? What do we really believe and furthermore how do we express that belief. *If we say those words and believe it, then we need to live like we do.* It is the very air that we breathe; it is that which fills us with new life – we are reminded of the words 'in him we live and move and have our being'.

A part of my ministry in the inner city is to facilitate the process whereby people can grow and become more confident in their faith. If we 'know' what we believe in, then we will not be afraid to live it and show it confidently! So how do I do this?

I meet with parishioners individually and in small groups to pray and study the Scriptures. When people come for baptism (as they think they have a right to), there is baptism preparation. In spending time with them (two to three sessions plus a final meeting with the godparents), I use the opportunity to share the gospel with them.

Through the occasional offices, we meet with people on a regular basis. As clergy we need to use these opportunities. All our parishioners have friends and acquaintances outside the church. We need to find a way of helping them to talk comfortably about their faith with those around them: in the pub, at the cinema or wherever we socialize.

But intellectual engagement alone is inadequate. Of course it is not helped if we say to our own under-aged children that they don't need to attend worship! Are we not sending them the wrong signals? After all, worship is something we do together. Worship is an integral part of our being confident Christians. Amidst all the pain and brokenness around us in the inner city our worship needs to be vibrant and meaningful. It is the interface with the unchurched community at large. When they walk through the doors, our worship must tell them who we are and what we are about. The music, the message, and the fellowship can be a determining factor as to whether others are drawn to make that connection.

We have hidden for long enough behind the covering of being shy or reserved. Remember, 'God has not given us the Spirit of timidity and fear, but of power and of love and a sound mind' (2 Timothy 1.7).

Cultural awareness

Secondly, to participate in evangelism in the inner city, we need to be consciously aware of the cultural diversity present around us. We find in our inner cities people from working class and from minority ethnic backgrounds.

This provides us with a great challenge to go out and build deliberate links with the different communities; building links of friendships; building lines of communication and trust. Instead we very often sit back and hope that 'they' will come to us.

When we have built up these links, we will need to consciously tap into and make use of the diverse cultural and human resources around us. If our minority ethnic population feel they have a stake within the fellowship, they will not only embrace it, but allow themselves to be embraced by it. For black people, our faith is not practised in a vacuum. The positive building of relationships is fertile ground for witnessing to one's faith.

Social outreach

The third aspect of doing evangelism in the inner city has to do with social outreach. John Crysostom, Bishop of Constantinople (c. 347-407) spoke of two altars. One in the sanctuary of the temple and the other in the market place.

As we share our eucharistic bread in the temple, we must also share our food and our existence with our neighbours in the market place. The two altars are not mutually exclusive. *'Their story must become our story.'* Like the women who journeyed with our Lord on the way to the cross, we too must journey with those around us and those who are on the fringe of society; those in need; those around us who are shunned. The churches (where they are) must be willing to be their voice, to be a part of the process whereby they are empowered to regain their voices.

There is a challenge for us to step outside of our comfortable existence and to enter the fray as we seek to point out injustices. When Mosely used to stand on his soapbox in Dalston market in the East end, a local congregation would often get there before him with the purpose of sharing an alternative message of love with the market shoppers.

Conclusion

If we are going to do evangelism in the inner city, then we must be confident in the gospel. We must equip our congregations confidently to share what the Holy Spirit has done and is doing.

We must be willing to reach out into the various communities (black and white). We must approach these communities not only with humility but with the realization that we have something to learn from them too.

And finally, we must be willing to walk alongside those on the fringes of society. In doing so we will be living out the gospel (this in itself is great evangelism!).

Rose Hudson-Wilkin *is a parish priest in East London. Previously she was a Diocesan Officer for Black Anglican Concerns (Lichfield Diocese) in the West Midlands, and a priest in an inner-city parish. She has also been a link person for the Committee for Minority Ethnic Anglican Concerns and a member of the General Synod.*

What Evangelism Means to Me

Henri Orombi

I want to say that I am so delighted to be at this conference and to have such a warmth of welcome and a beautiful time of fellowship with you. I have been catching up with my old friends as well, which is a joy to me. I am thrilled also to be among Anglicans who are serious about mission and evangelism.

The first time I came into this country was 19 years ago. I came to study at St John's Nottingham. I was sponsored by Holy Trinity, Brompton, a church that was already growing and in which God was at work. I found that this country is a very peculiar country and I'll tell you why. I was catapulted from the centre of Africa (Uganda is almost in the middle), to the centre of the world in London. I walked out on my first morning. I was staying with a curate in St Paul's, Onslow Square in South Kensington. I walked along a small path, and I began saying 'Good morning' to people. The first person I said 'Good morning' to just looked at me and just walked past. The next person I said 'Good morning' to never even looked at me. I kept on walking along the road and was beginning to wonder 'What do these people think I'm asking for?' So I went back to my friend and I said, 'Don't these people receive greetings?' and he said to me, 'Henri, you are not in Uganda, this is London,' and I learnt my first lesson.

On my very first Sunday I went to church at Holy Trinity, Brompton and the church was full and vibrant and warm, the fellowship was fantastic and I felt I was in Uganda – I was at home. There were a lot of praise songs. I didn't know many of them but I was enjoying singing. Then the very next Sunday I went to Sussex to a place I'll not mention. I went to a church with my friend. We went in and people began to filter in but the church was not filling up and I was beginning to wonder if this was the same England. At the end of the service I counted. I took a count of the congregation and there were exactly twelve people and a dog. I was surprised, I must tell you, I was very surprised. In one place the church is packed, in another place there is hardly anybody there; the buildings are there, the pews are there, everything is there. And I wondered what was happening.

Finally, when I went to St John's, I had the shock of my life. In St John's I learnt a spirituality I was not familiar with. Back home, in my church, my people are noisy people; we make a lot of noise. We make noise in church; we make noise in the villages; we are so noisy; and in St John's on a Wednesday morning, from after breakfast to 11 o'clock, everything is expected to be quiet. You see what I mean? I walked from the dining hall and as I was coming to check letters at the pigeon holes, I met an English student there and I whispered, I didn't talk aloud but just whispered, 'Good Morning'. He wouldn't even answer me, and I got so frustrated, I went to my room, picked up my guitar and played and sang for 30 minutes, to drown my frustration.

England has never ceased to amaze me. I arrived on Saturday at Gatwick and I was told it was already beginning to be spring, so I wasn't very warmly dressed. The pilot first of all warned us that it was three degrees and a bit chilly for those coming from Uganda, because when we left Kampala it was 30 degrees, warm and hot. I arrived in London and it was cold and windy, and then we drove up to Nottingham and what did I see? – snow! Beloved friends, I am so glad to be back in England! This morning God in his mercy even made the temperature kind to me. In fact, as I was singing I was sweating, and I said, 'God is good.' The Church of England is to me the taproot and trunk of my church. Although some very unusual things happen to me, there is always something I will remember, and that is that God brought very special people into my life.

I remember being interviewed in Holy Trinity, Brompton and the question that I was asked was, 'What do you hope to achieve by being in England?' I said, 'If I can make friends in England, I will have achieved a great deal.' Would you believe it, after three years I was asked the same question, 'What do you think you have achieved by being in England?' And I remembered my first answer, 'Well as I told you last time, I have my friends and I want to give thanks for the gift of friendship based on the love of God. This has maintained the relationship between me and my brothers and sisters in England up to this time, and I come here and meet two or three of them who have meant a lot to me over the years. To me that is the gospel – that we love because he first loved us.'

But let me give a little insight into my church. You may not know this history so let me bring it to you. In the last century explorers went to look for the source of the Nile, and they came to my country and they named the river the Nile. They came to a huge lake, which they share with Tanzania and Kenya, and they named it after the queen of the last century, Queen

Victoria. As the explorers were coming back the king of the place where they arrived by the shores of Lake Victoria made a request. He said, 'Can you please go back to your queen and tell her to send missionaries to us?' And in 1877 missionaries braved all the problems of travelling in their time. Today we can jet for eight hours and arrive in London, and then you can do the same and you arrive in Nebbi. The missionaries took weeks and came to us, in a time when there were no proper roads, no railway, there were wild animals and even the people in the tribes were wild. Tropical diseases were multitude. Love of God motivated these people from England to travel all the way to my own country to the palace of this king, and they began to proclaim the gospel.

Church of England, you mean a lot to us. You know about Africa in these years. You called it the Dark Continent, not because the sun doesn't shine in Africa – the sun is there all the time, twelve hours a day and seven days a week. But the darkness was there because we did not know God the Father of our Lord Jesus Christ. We had some knowledge about God but it was hazy. And these missionaries came and brought the gospel to us. And as they planted the gospel in the court of the king, a number of his servants embraced it, and they began to believe. They were baptized and the gospel began to spread. It was not long before the king died and his son took over and began to kill the believers. Right from the beginning the Church of Uganda passed through fire and persecution. The people who embraced the gospel were mutilated, they were burnt, they were killed, they were destroyed. He wanted to stamp out Christianity right from the start. My Church was born by fire brought to us by your people from England.

Now I have been listening to you and hear that some of you are pretty discouraged about the state of affairs in the Church of England, so some of you probably find this a bit heavy going. I just want to say to you – 'Don't be discouraged!' You took the gospel to us and I have come back as a product of that gospel. The first fire was a fire or persecution. Each year on 3 June, we commemorate the people who died for their faith, and we thank God for them because a number of them were young people who went into the fire rejoicing and singing, because they thought they were counted worthy to die for the cause of the gospel and for Christ. You know your history. It has been said by a bishop that the blood of martyrs is a seed of the gospel. As people died, the fire of the gospel spread and the number of people embracing it began to multiply. That is the beginning of my Church.

Another fire came in the 1930s. In the 1930s in Rwanda, the fire was lit which was called the East African Revival. That was a fire of revival. The Holy Spirit breathed upon this church. Incidentally, the Church of England and its structures is a hindrance to mission. It seems that when the Church begins to get too structured, and things are set in place and become routine, people begin to organize God, but God refuses to be organized. And so there has been some lukewarmness, even if people had died for their faith, until the Holy Spirit began to breathe upon my country. People met together to share and to pray, and the Holy Spirit came. Let me remind you that mission and evangelism without the urgency of the Holy Spirit is a lot of wasted time and money. When the Holy Spirit began to convict people, they began to confess their sins. They sat together and opened up their hearts. The Lord bypassed the clergy and went to the lay people and the lay people sat together and could see the fire of the revival coming. It began burning in Rwanda, came into Uganda, over to Tanzania and into Kenya and the East African Revival continues. Friends, I am a product of the East African Revival; the late Archbishop Janani Luwum was a product of that East African revival. I praise God for the East African Revival. And incidentally, there were some British also involved in it!

But such a movement is bound to be tested. In 1971, the political fire came. The brutal Amin government came to power. Amin was semi-literate and a soldier, but he came to power in a very tricky way. We didn't believe a man like Amin could come to power, let alone rule for eight years, but he did. And those were years of darkness and years of pain. Our country was disintegrating, things just collapsed – our civil service, our structures and our economy. Amin's rule was a tragedy, and as a church we were also part and parcel of that. Amin killed a lot of intellectuals; many had to flee. He targeted the church. I was one of the victims.

I once went to Entebbe, where the international airport is, to encourage the believers. I went into a home and people gathered. We spent a good time talking. We talked and we had lunch, and as I was about to go, they said 'Please can you share the word with us?' I said, 'Certainly,' and I took my Bible and opened it at John 15: 'I am the vine and you are the branches.' I began to read from verses 1-5, and just as I finished verse 5, the soldiers and secret police walked into the house. They had been watching us and we were arrested. I said 'But I am a student. I come from the theological college,' but unfortunately my ID was in my jacket which I had hung up on the wall. I had no way to get it. They arrested us and put us in the police station and accused us falsely, as they do to believers. They said the people were organizing a political meeting and they are people from a church that the government has burnt, and we were stripped to remove everything. There were eleven people, seven men and four women, locked in different cells. They put us in such small cells that if I lay on my back, my feet would be on one wall and my head on the other, and there was no way I could stretch myself. There was nothing to lie on; we were denied water and we were not given the opportunity to go even to the loo. Every evening people were beaten and killed and we could hear the agony and the pain. The following morning they brought up a man who had only stolen a bunch of bananas, just a bunch of bananas. They put him out in the corridor. They began beating up this man in front of us, and they beat him so badly that his skin broke and blood was soaking his pants and the man was crying and pleading for mercy, and we had to watch. They just wanted us to see it. I wasn't a criminal, I wasn't guilty of anything. I began to understand that you don't have to be a criminal to go to prison. I began to understand that the gospel itself has such a power that people will resist it.

The church suffered with all Ugandans, during the brutal and unstable leadership of 1971. Many of the clergy either left the ministry or compromised their faith. The economic hardship was so great that Christians were also into the black market and we sank very low morally, and many capable leaders went underground. Would one evangelize at a time like this? When things are so hard, is it easy to evangelize? When you are being targeted and followed all the time, can you evangelize? Shouldn't evangelism take place in a time when things are good and easy and nice – like your time, for example? You have the telephone, you have the fax, you have email, you have television, you have meals, you have your cars, you have the railways, you have air travel. Shouldn't this be the time when we evangelize? Was it possible for us to evangelize at that time? Let me tell you – yes, it was! As the church we remained faithful and spoke against brutality, and our leaders paid heavily for that.

Would Amin have the guts to arrest the archbishop of the whole church of Uganda and Rwanda? – he did. Two weeks before he was arrested and killed, soldiers went into his home and cut through the fence. He opened the door and there were men standing there who they beat him with a gun and did all kinds of things. They took him to every room in the house and they said, 'Get us the guns.' And those of you who knew Janani Luwum know that he was such a man of God. He held up his Bible and said, 'I don't have guns – this is my God,' and they left him. Half the bishops met and they made an appeal to the World Council of Churches and the Anglican Consultative Council. Amin became wild and the archbishop was killed in cold blood. Why? Let me tell you something. The gospel is so important that when the archbishop's wife asked, 'Janani, why don't you leave, why don't you go to England, why don't you go elsewhere?' this is what he replied. 'To whom will I leave the ship? If I run away where is the safety of my people?' He chose to be with these people, with his church.

As you have been talking over the week, I have heard you speak of the importance of having leaders whose hearts go out to the people in mission and evangelism. At this point the Church begins to sort out its priorities and friends. If you get arrested and go to prison, you go to preach. Paul and Peter did the same, they took the gospel there. Paul once declared that the word of God is not chained and it became evident in our Church. Friends that is the background of my Church and I think I have bored you enough. Let me get to the Decade of Evangelism, as I wind up my talk.

The Decade of Evangelism began in 1988, and this is how I see it. It may be subjective, but I want to encourage you by what God the Father of our Lord Jesus Christ can do in evangelism. I came to understand that God is interested in evangelism. The Decade of Evangelism came when I asked my bishop to make me an archdeacon! I asked to go to a very difficult place, a very run-down place with people whose self-esteem was next to nothing. The place was so remote; it is still remote. Power lines were installed only last year; there is no running water; the people were suffering from isolation. I asked the bishop, 'Can I go there?' partly because I was young and adventurous and also because I always love to see places where God can work. So he said, 'You go', and I went. The Holy Spirit inspired me. First of all, God gave me a Land Rover! And then I mounted horn speakers on that Land Rover and I got an amplifier and a player and I began travelling up and down the place. Now this was one archdeaconry, which is now the diocese of Nebbi, and I would go up and down playing Christian music. As I drove around people would know for miles that Henri was coming! One day my brother told me straight. He said, 'Our area is not safe and you display yourself and warn your enemies from so far away with all this music.' I said, 'It is better that they kill me when they know it's me, than kill me by mistake!'

God knows his people and he knows how to communicate with them. At this point he told me to put up horn speakers. I only know horn speakers and music like that from the ice-cream vans in England and I became like one of them. It was pretty stupid, I think, for an archdeacon to do that. But it is through stupid things that sometimes God can work, because as we preached the gospel – we were preaching the real gospel, the good news which is based on the love of God for his people – the Lord began to stir the hearts of people. We began to train musicians in evangelistic methods and they could use their music to communicate as a vehicle for communicating the gospel. These were young men and women and some older people. They used brass instruments because they did not need amplification and they would go out into places and stand up and play gospel music and the crowds would come, and when they came we preached.

The gospel is dynamic, as Paul said. He said, 'I am not ashamed of the gospel, for it is the power of God to salvation.' Now sometimes when I listen to you, I think you are a little too complicated in your gospel communication. I believe that the gospel has been made simple by God through the incarnation. I believe that God wanted the gospel to be simple but not simplistic. God wanted the gospel to be so simple that we never misunderstand it, and so we preach the simple gospel – 'Jesus loves you'. Jesus loves me and this I know, because the Bible says so.

We began to see prayer groups springing up. I'm glad that Bishop Nigel mentioned prayer. Dotted around in parishes, prayer groups began to spring up. And do you know who they are targeting? They were targeting leaders; they were targeting the clergy and the lay leaders to pray for them, that they might have a vision, that they might be encouraged because, and I want to believe this, as a bishop and as a leader you get more criticisms than encouragement. Some of these criticisms are so baseless that you feel so discouraged and you don't know why. I'll tell you why. They are after you because actually they love you. The groups were praying for the leadership and they prayed for the leadership and, beloved friends, the Lord began to speak to the people.

Let me give you one example. I was having a morning devotion with my staff as an archdeacon and as we finished the morning devotion, one of my men put up his hand and said, 'Can I speak?' and I said, 'Certainly'. He said, 'Last night I had a dream and I dreamt that I was being taken and thrown in the lake of fire, but I could only remember one name and that was the name of Jesus, so I called the name of Jesus and was delivered.' He added, 'I need Jesus this morning,' and then he dug his hand in his pocket and pulled out cigarettes and all kinds of junk and charms. He said, 'I do not need this, I need Jesus. I have lots at home, can you please come and help me?' We closed our offices and went down to the village because there was somebody who needed Christ. He got out all the junk that he was using for his worship, and we put them on the fire and we began to praise God over the victory of Jesus Christ. And as we were singing a drunk (I don't know where he had been drinking because this was about 9.10 in the morning) came from one direction. He was staggering as he walked and he fell on his knees. He said, 'I also need Jesus.' We prayed for him to help him to know Christ, and another drunk from another direction appeared. Now three people in a day is not bad business!

The Word of God began to influence and affect our people as they prayed, and I would like to say that prayer indeed is essential in evangelism. We have discovered too that evangelistic ministry and mission is not for special people. You don't have to go to college and earn a degree, No, the Lord begins to move among his people. It is so important for us to know Jesus Christ, to know him, to be passionate about him, to do anything for him and to give yourself to him because he gave himself to you. In fact, back in my diocese, a pastor is required to give a testimony before he can stand and preach. When you are passionate about Jesus Christ then you can sell the gospel to friends. Who would ever refuse to introduce his wife to someone? I love my wife, I introduce my wife, I am proud of my wife. And if I love Jesus Christ, why am I not proud about Jesus? Why don't I get excited about him? Most ordinary people can be evangelistic. In fact in evangelism we are talking about where the church ought to be mobilized and the whole question of witnessing to, and talking about the message. Talk around about Jesus Christ and leave the result to God. Some of us get into difficulties because we are afraid of being embarrassed. Why not, get embarrassed about Jesus? But what if they don't listen to me? It isn't your problem. You asked to share, if nothing happens, God is concerned; if something happens, glory to him, and praise the Lord for that.

So now what we have is a situation where God has picked people not only from the diocese but he has also brought us Koreans. I have three Koreans on my staff. He has also brought us some English people. I have four English on my staff. He has brought for us a German as well. Now all these people are motivated by the love of God to share in the gospel and the ministry in my diocese of Nebbi is being shared. Let me remind you again, God is not looking for special people, God is looking for those who are willing to be his. As a ministry of evangelistic outreach we are also extending our services to the sick and to the needy. We have health clinics where, in the name of Jesus Christ, we dispense medicine, where we diagnose, treat, and teach people how they should live. In fact, I use a phrase from English (I don't know where I got it from) but I say that cleanliness is next to godliness, or something like that. Now I use that saying very, very much, that if you have God pass it on and love God and then you need to be clean. It is not very expensive to be clean. It is fun to give projects to people to empower them to know how they can live. As a Church we are responsible for injecting hope and self-esteem into the people, and lots of people can see the gospel being preached, not only in the pulpit, but also out among them. They have begun to see the holistic approach of the gospel. I am encouraging my women. I am one of those pro-women bishops who notice the power of women's ministry. I don't debate about ordination of women because it is immaterial to me. I organize my women and I release them and say, 'You go and minister.' I am looking for girls to ordain to come and help me. I also am encouraging young people, especially girls, by educating them. I raise funds and I pay their school fees and these girls, I believe, will become women and these women will be powerful agents for change in my diocese and my country. I believe it is my responsibility as a bishop to empower these people to reflect Jesus Christ, and God is helping us.

What have we witnessed? We have witnessed the numerical growth of our church. In 1988, we had 24 parishes in this place, now we have 35 parishes. We have 300 congregations here. In 1988, we had only one archdeaconry, now we have four archdeaconries and a deanery. The prayer ministry has developed to a point now, as I speak, where the diocese has built a prayer retreat centre. We call it the prayer mountain because we went and touched the whole mountain and built a chapel which can seat between 800 and 1000 people. I don't believe in cathedrals but I believe in prayer places, so I haven't started building a cathedral yet. We are encouraging people to come and pray, and they go and pray and fast there. Back in my own society the Anglican Church did not know what fasting was but they knew what feasting was. Now we talk about feasting to fasting.

It is so important that we pray and see God's face that God may give us direction in our ministry. What does God want to tell us, what does God want us to do? I am beginning to feel that I have talked a bit too much now. But I believe that this prayer mountain that we have developed is not only for my diocese but for my nation. People come from Kampala and come to seek the face of God, the Church as a diocese is also beginning to build a training centre because we would like to train leaders. We are desperately in need of leaders; in fact, I am even on a recruiting mission here. If you believe and you feel God is calling you to come, please do come to Nebbi and we can use you to teach our people.

We have seen some problems; it isn't all sunshine and roses. We have seen three problems. Our biggest problem is discipleship. Many are coming to Jesus Christ and they can remain converts rather than disciples. We are challenged to get strategic materials to disciple our believers that they may not be tossed about by every wind of doctrine which they come across, which is very easy these days. Then secondly, we are faced with another challenge to teach our Christians to be responsible for the Church and the mission movement of the Church. We have been too dependent on the Church in England and America and now in Asia. We want to begin to say that we the Church in Africa must begin to learn how to depend on ourselves. We are also now beginning to say it is time for us to look beyond our borders, because if you people didn't come to us, you would not receive the gospel. Similarly we now need to take the gospel elsewhere.

Finally, I come to the last fire that I see in my diocese as we now move on from the Decade of Evangelism. At the moment, our biggest fire which is getting into our country and our nation is Islam. I think this is also the case here in England. Islam has become bold and aggressive today in Uganda, and why must Christians stand by with folded arms? I tell my Christians about the rise of the Church of Christ and tell the story which has never grown old. Because our gospel is Jesus Christ, saviour of the whole world, we preach Christ and not ourselves, Paul says. And today, Christ must be proclaimed by his Church. Paul meant it. It worries me if I do not preach the gospel. We believe that the only thing that can move forward and hold the advance of Islam which is coming from the Arab countries, is the Word of God preached and the Word of God taught and for believers to know their faith. I believe that if you do that, you will not be tempted by money or by marriage because they use both in my country. They pick our girls (they don't allow us to pick their girls) and when they pick our girls they must become Muslims. So we are saying to our young women, if you haven't found a husband, seek one from the Lord and the Lord will give to you. We are helping our Christians to understand that.

The other challenge you are receiving right now is the challenge of materialism. It is the same in my country as it is here. The world has become so small that everything that happens in London in the morning, by the evening is in Kampala. The email, the Internet, the fax and television, CNN, BBC, are all in Kampala. The materialistic approach to living that you are seeing has also impinged on us. But didn't Jesus Christ say that you should seek first the kingdom of God and all these other things would be added to you. God knows we need all these things but should the Church spend all her time seeking for these other things at the expense of her mission, which does not take first place in many churches? The answer is: no. Therefore, my brothers and sisters, we are taking risks because God also took risks to trust us with his holy gospel. The voice of the gospel rings out loud and clear: Whom shall I send? Who will go for us? He desires that we get involved in going for him and as it was then, so it is now. Here I am, send me Lord, even me. And now to him who alone sits at the Father's right hand, interceding for the militant church, be glory and honour now and for evermore. Amen.

Henri Orombi *is the Bishop of Nebbi in Uganda.*

3

Reports from the Tracks
and Base Group Programmes

The Tracks Programme

The Tracks Programme was designed to equip participants with the vision, ideas and skills to do evangelism into the new Millennium. The sessions were practical and future-orientated using the experience of those participating. Each Track was asked to submit a report of their sessions. The following are their reports.

EVANGELISM AND CHILDREN

- The centre of all is the figure of the living God, we resource a real and authentic spirituality in children fed by sacramental love and action.

- Is there any difference between evangelizing adults and evangelizing children? Liturgy, love and prayer speak.

- We (the Body of Christ) need children and are impoverished without children. They demand a voice, empowerment and respect.

- Children have a right to be introduced to God – their inheritance.

- Children as evangelists – can we feed our children with full sacramental resources of the Church: Eucharist, grace and full privileges of membership.

- Liturgy for children: this is liturgy for those who are marginalized in various parts of the church.

- We must explore the dynamic between nurture and evangelism.

- Story telling/parable is a simple yet profound tool.

- We must enable children to enjoy and own the whole of Scripture.

- Ask the children what concerns them.

ARTS IN EVANGELISM AND MISSION

- God is fun and engages our hearts and our hands in creative learning.

- It is important we explore every way of doing things.

- It is important for the Church to recognize and encourage excellence amongst gifted artists.

- We need to use the gifts and talents we have in evangelism and mission which will release further gifts.

- Creativity and spontaneity needs to be the norm in worship.

- As a Track we are appalled at the addiction to words apparent at this conference.

PROCESS EVANGELISM

- Becoming a Christian is like a journey.

- The missionary Church needs to find ways of accompanying people on the journey.

Therefore as a Church we need:

- Programmes of training in the process of evangelism, and the available resources and models at every level of church life.

- Realize the evangelistic potential of all we do.

- Further develop collaborative patterns of ministry.

- Make sure the language of journey is evident in our liturgy.

- Enable Christian people to fulfil their apostolic vocation.

Also

- The journey of faith is a life-long journey:
    - Do we recognize the faith of children?
    - Will we let them evangelize us?

- We need to *be* evangelistic – not 'Go' and make disciples, but *as you go*.

- And finally, when it comes to the process of evangelism it is good to be the Church of England – we have so many opportunities!

WOMEN'S TRACK – ROOTS AND ROUTES

As the Church entering the new millennium:

Actively seek to live out Jesus' model of relating to women:

- – intimacy and friendship;
- – giving respect and responsibility;
- – accepting both emotion and intellect.

Commit ourselves to enabling children, women and men to reach their full potential.

Equalize numerical representation in every context.

SPIRITUALITY – THE HEART OF EVANGELISM

The subject was addressed under three headings:

- Spirituality and the individual – personal renewal;
- Spirituality and the Church – corporate renewal;
- 'What is truth?' – spirituality and theology.

Affirmations:

- Personal and sustained encounter with God through Jesus Christ, to evangelize effectively is vitally important.

- Adopt a veni, vidi, velcro ('stick at it') spirituality in the Church.

- We share grace and God's gift to us in Christ – not guilt or fear.

- Sustained encounter with God is key, redeeming the whole of life.

- Jesus is truth – the sum total of all reality.

- Scripture is the plumb-line for our spirituality.

- We discern Christ's truth in other situations and religions: but affirm that he was and is the unique Lamb of God sacrificed once for all.

- We are called to *life*, not religion.

- Renewal is something that happens to you, by God's grace: and is not something to do or make.

- Spirituality is engagement with both the transcendent and the material.

Recommendations:

- That all clergy and other Church leaders should submit themselves to spiritual direction.

- That the primary task of the bishops and clergy is to teach people to pray, and lead them in prayer.

- That the Church should set aside power and discover weakness.

- That the Church should do fewer things better.

- That the PCC agenda should major on spirituality.

THE WORLD CHURCH AND EVANGELISM IN ENGLAND

- We recognized the great expansion of the Church in this century, but our experience showed that we had found help from Christians of many cultures both 'north' and 'south'.

- The undergirding principle the group identified was that of the 'mutuality of the Churches of the world in the gospel'. We need to support, encourage and learn from each other.

- Our aim will be to find culturally relevant ways boldly and joyfully to make Christ known.

- There is value in hearing and seeing the faith expressed and lived out in unfamiliar ways.

- To enable this mutuality in the gospel to grow, relationships between Churches worldwide need to be strengthened.

- This is best done through the experience of people meeting people and working with them. People are the priority.

- The practical expressions of this for the Church of England are its world mission agencies, diocesan links and the connections of individuals and parish, both within the Anglican Communion and ecumenically.

- Exchange of people, sending and receiving, particularly groups of people, faith-sharing teams and the like is important.

- The importance of giving *young people* experience of the Church overseas was stressed.

- Clergy secondments were mentioned.

- Christians of different and ethnic backgrounds within our churches need to be recognized and affirmed.

- In this mutual support in the gospel we need always to be ready for the surprise, the note of joy, the unexpected.

REACHING MEN IN MILLENNIUM 3

Three questions were addressed:

1. What have been the main social influences on men over the last 50 years?

2. What are the issues the Church faces in evangelizing men?

3. In the light of (1) and (2), how can the Church best reach men today?

1. The main influences noted were:

- The changing patterns in working life (who is the breadwinner etc.);

- The changing patterns in domestic arrangements (e.g. gender roles, marriage, cohabitation, divorce, etc.);

- A significant increase in uncertainty about male roles (work, home, gay issues, etc.);

- Greater possibility of platonic friendships with women.

2. Issues in evangelizing men:

- The image of the Church and of Christian men is often feminine.

- We are using outdated evangelistic styles, often over cerebral, often ignoring networks.

- Do we create spaces where issues of identity and self-worth can be safely addressed?

- There is a problem in contemporary Britain over male identity.

- Time pressures, i.e. fragmentation.

3.   Pointers to the future (NB: not necessarily unique to men):

●   Learn from the model of Jesus, in all its facets.

●   Incarnational relationships are developed around common tasks.

●   Watch the language of worship(!).

●   Equip people for sharing faith at work.

●   Start with topic of common interest, rather than doctrine.

●   Provide an image of Christian role models.

TRANSFORMING THE LOCAL CHURCH IN MISSION

Ways into mission mode

These are some of the ways in which our Churches are making the journey from Church in 'inherited mode' to Church in 'mission mode'. For those involved in churches, or called on to help churches, these are the things to watch out for and to point to as ways forward.

●   Asking purposeful questions – What are we trying to do here? What is the best way of doing it?

●   Engaging in mission – mission activities in the community, Church focusing on being a reflection of the gospel by the way they operate. Equip members to function in a Christian manner in dispersed mode.

●   Addressing spirituality of both the community and the Church. And personal spirituality.

●   Doing a thorough job of initiation helping people on journey of faith and also for existing members.

●   New beginnings – Church 'beginning again', e.g. through church planting, cell churches, etc.

●   Helping churches to address the question of where they are going and what the next steps are to getting there.

●   Parish/church/mission audit/surveys growth area at present. Ask questions, set goals, aims direction which can be monitored and evaluated.

- Addressing church growth – what is causing that growth, and how can it be multiplied and passed on to other churches?

Healthy churches – characteristics

- The 'Durham' marks

Presenting causes

- an enabling style of leadership;

- a participative style of laity;

- openness to change;

- the use of small groups;

- an outward looking ethos;

- a clear vision, and shared sense of direction;

- doing a quality job.

Preparatory causes

- enthusiasm;

- building of confidence (breaking clergy dependency, etc.);

- strong community links (high visibility of the church, effective pastoral care, etc.).

Underlying cause

It is the reality of the Church's encounter with God (sometimes, but by no means always, starting with the incumbent) which is what motivates:

- clergy to adopt an enabling style of leadership;

- laity to have something with which to participate, namely their awareness of the reality of God;

- congregations to be ready to face the need for, and willing to pay the price of change;

- churches to be outward looking, because they have been touched by God's compassion and feel called into mission;

- churches to discover a sense of direction that comes from their desire to discover and reveal more of God's nature;

Everyone to be committed to doing a quality job.

Natural church development (Christian Schwarz) characteristics

1. Empowering leadership;
2. Gift orientated lay ministry;
3. Passionate spirituality;
4. Functional structures;
5. Inspiring worship services;
6. Holistic small groups;
7. Need-orientated evangelism;
8. Loving relationships.

PRACTISING GOOD NEWS TO THE POOR

Who are the poor?	Those increasingly facing social exclusion.
Why the good news?	Luke 4.18-19
What is the good news?	Safety, security, hope, freedom, relationships, regeneration that is economically sustainable.
Where do we share it?	We live the gospel by living it with our neighbour, schools work, community involvement at all levels where people are.
How do we share it?	Not kicking people when they are down;
	Listening, walking alongside;
	Discovering quality people called to save the poor (not those dumped by the Church);
	Providing role models for leadership;

Allowing/enabling/equipping people to take
responsibility for their lives;

Community issues, social action.

When do we share it?   Occasional offices, feast days, celebrations,
day trips, outings, after-school clubs.

Luke 4.18-19

Issues   The poor are getting poorer;

Increasingly facing social exclusion.

Tensions of clergy living in parishes, being
part of the community but should we be
rethinking models of parochial ministry for
some areas/situations?

Where is the vocation to serve the poor?

How do we encourage those serving in
these areas?

How can diocesan structures

1.   relieve burdens of quota payments;

2.   facilitate and equip parishes which
       will not give instant success stories;

3.   meet the need for increasing skills
       and support in applying for
       government funding/community
       development?

Who will listen to our stories?

MAKING THE MOST OF THE MILLENNIUM

The Millennium is a 'gift' to us to make Jesus known:

●   We can't postpone it.

●   It's an opportunity.

●   The Millennium is not the Dome!

●   It's about Jubilee.

Last year's Gallup poll discovered only one out of six people know that the Millennium is connected to Jesus of Nazareth.

In response the churches have decided on a mission statement – 'to forge a link in people's minds beyond the year 2000, between the name of Jesus and the possibility of personal meaning and public hope that he offers to all'.

NewStart is offered to help us do this. There are three messages:

NewStart for the world's poor;

         at home;

         with God.

There is a great range of initiatives and resources to help us achieve a way of forging the link in people's minds.

The six we particularly looked at were:

●   The CTE candle initiative and resolution;

●   The Millennium Gospels;

●   Fanfare – a challenge to the nation to return to church on 2 January;

●   Y-2000 – a way of making Jesus known through using a simple picture of an ancient symbol.

●   The Jesus Video Project – putting the story of Jesus into every home.

The group felt that churches should seriously get on board now and not delay. Don't think too big. Choose two or three initiatives, pray and do those exceedingly well!

YOUTH EVANGELISM

There are three recommendations from the Youth Track:

1. A fund should be set up for new initiatives in evangelism amongst young people. This could be administered much in the same way as the Church Urban Fund. It would need to be ongoing in the Church of England's annual budget. We suggest £1 million would be a good start.

2. Every deanery should develop at least one evangelism project among young people within five years. Imagination and risk taking should be encouraged here (e.g. a church on the Internet, schools worker, deanery youth cell network, youth congregation, a night-club as a base for relational work, etc.).

    We particularly highlight the need for developing strong commitments of faith among young people.

3. The institutional Church has a big role to play in legitimizing or giving its blessing to these new endeavours. We need to move from a deficit model to one of equal partnership.

EQUIPPING THE CHURCH TO TELL GOD'S STORY

'Jesus was not a theologian, he was God who told stories.'

(*Madeleine l'Engle*)

This was a great Track because storytelling is:

- easy to learn;
- great evangelistic and teaching tool;
- enormous fun.

Mesmerizing:
- hearing stories;
- visual;
- everyone loves a good story.

Visionary:

- bridges religious/secular divide;
- non manipulative.

Scope for creativity:

- works alongside other forms, e.g. music, liturgy and drama;
- very user-friendly in venues from pubs to churches to hospices to families.

'God made people because he loves stories.'

(Hasidic saying)

PERSONALITY AND COMMUNICATING THE GOSPEL

- There is still a long way to go in helping people to discover their unique, God-given way of communicating their faith.
- There are many different models and aspects to communicating the gospel.
- When communicating the gospel to one another we hear more than words.
- In teams there is a constant need to work with different personality types present. We are one body but with many parts. Our unity is in diversity.
- Evangelism is dialogue.
- There is a danger of some personality types controlling churches or groups and then self-perpetuating unless people are prepared to be open and work constructively with their differences.

INFORMATION TECHNOLOGY – BRAVE NEW WORLD

- Is the Internet the sort of place Christians should be? – Yes.

- Who should run web sites? – Parishes, individuals, families, denominations, dioceses and organizations.

- A web site is a considerable investment in terms of money, time and regular commitment.

- Remember reciprocal linkings of resource web sites.

- Use the Web wisely.

The Base Group Programme

The Base Group Programme consisted of 28 groups of between ten to twelve people. They met three times during ACE '99 to work, pray, discuss and study together. The purpose of these groups was to provide a place where participants could belong, challenge, ask questions and have fun. Each Base Group had a leader and a recorder whose role was to ensure that the concerns of the group were fed into the main conference process. The statements and questions below are a reflection of those discussions.

Issues concerning evangelism

- Remember the importance of the use of buildings in evangelism.

- Believing *follows* belonging.

- Where are the youth at this conference? Where are the black delegates?

- It is important to understand the *process* of evangelism which enables us to be more appropriate and effective in sharing the gospel.

- Evangelism is all about risk.

- The strength of mission is recognizing Christian diversity and using that diversity to evangelize to a whole community with all its needs and wants.

- The way we evangelize needs to be open, honest and real – about the good and bad points.

- There is a need to go on asking critical theological questions about mission – recognizing that there is a difference between mission and evangelism.

- 'As the Father has sent me so I have sent you' – this is an essential theological undergirding for every congregation.

- Begin with the Word – not words. Communicate the gospel with all-in incarnational mission.

- Are we prepared to learn from the world church given their experience and apparent success in evangelism?

- How do we evaluate the Decade of Evangelism when the words 'mission' and 'evangelism' are used interchangeably?

- Do we have a definition of evangelism?

- Have integrity in all we do – walk the talk.

- Holistic mission is essential and we want to endorse prophetic evangelism as a key part of this.

- There is a need to keep working at where we go next so that we do not lose the gains of the Decade of Evangelism.

- Each church grouping needs the insights of the others to share the faith. None of us has all the truth!

- We are needing a greater depth of study on the issues being addressed – e.g. theological base of evangelism, dynamics of conversion etc.

- The majority of people at the conference seem to be middle class – we need recognition across the board – working class, inner city etc.

- It is necessary to recognize older people – there are more early retired people in our churches.

- What is the theological purpose of mission and evangelism in the twenty-first century?

- How might we approach people who are content with life and who have no spiritual thirst?

- Where are we learning to talk the faith of the people outside the Church?

- Spirit-led incarnational evangelism is central.

- A Trinitarian God – how does this concept relate to people who are searching?

- We need to proclaim the gospel – sow seeds not persuade people to come to faith.

- Worship and evangelism go hand in hand.

- We need to emphasize again the importance of equipping the laity in evangelism.

- Awe, wonder, mystery, sign and symbol are all essential in evangelism.

- It is necessary to maintain the tension between encouragement and challenge.

- We should continually and prayerfully re-examine our real motives for evangelism.

- Please will clergy notice and encourage lay people who are not leaders?

Issues concerning young people and children

- Could a fund be endowed towards radical, imaginative youth work administered primarily by those with vision and involvement with youth so that they can 'catch the wave'?

- How are we equipping adult Christians to pass on their faith to children?

- Evangelism needs to be contextual.

- Children and young people are the key.

4

Personal Reflections

Elizabeth Mackey
Methodist representative

It was about a quarter past seven when I went into the chapel. There were already plenty of people there, mostly standing, though some were sitting on the floor or on chairs. People greeted each other with smiles but no words. A man standing near me murmured in my ear, 'I've been asked to help serve and to find two others. Will you serve the wine?' I gladly agreed. Little did I know! Coming from a tradition where the Communion wine is non-alcoholic, it never occurred to me that there might be a problem when we consumed the remainder of the elements after the service. As we stood, nine or ten of us in the tiny room serving as a sacristy, I looked at the large quantity of wine in the cup I held, then at the other people, solemnly consuming their remnants. I would have been glad of a piece of bread to help the wine on its way but nobody met my eye and I didn't like to break the silence. I took a deep breath and did my duty. As we crossed over to the dining room for breakfast, I felt decidedly light-headed – but perhaps it was the Holy Spirit, after all.

ACE '99, however, was much more than a lesson in boozing before breakfast. Perhaps the most enduring impression will be of the people there. All varieties of theology, churchmanship and understanding of the words 'evangelism' and 'mission' seem to have been represented. It could have been a week of contention and defensiveness. But it was far from that. Disagreement there was, but it was the dialectic of growth, not the heat of set ideas. People listened to one another. They sought to understand one another. The resulting atmosphere was very positive and encouraging. I was perhaps fortunate in that I belonged to a base group that 'worked' – people turned up when they were supposed to and contributed to the discussion. We got on well enough to be able to share some deeper concerns than the immediate issues of the conference and to feel comfortable in doing so. It was a shame that we only met three times (though perhaps other groups that didn't gel so well were relieved). The groups did, however, serve a purpose in breaking down barriers between strangers so that we were ready to talk about more than trivia as we met informally at meals and other breaks. This was important because one of the great values of the conference was the informal sharing – perhaps more than the formal sessions, though without the formality no one would have come.

As with many Christian conferences, ACE '99 could have been rather shorter if it had not been for all the worship, yet how else can we involve our God in our conference than by being in communication and communion with him? I heard grumbles about the music, about the disregard of Lent in the use of alleluias, about the use of an unlicensed liturgy . . . Personally, I found the worship mostly helpful. Coming from a tradition which shows its value of the Sacrament by rarer, rather than more frequent celebration, I found daily Eucharist a special blessing. The varied liturgies were no problem for me since Methodism allows much variety, though I was embarrassed that I did not know by heart the Creed and the Gloria. The non-sacramental services were good and especially the wordless liturgy of Thursday evening. A special blessing was to be able to meet and say office with other Companions of the Northumbria Community.

The workshops, the seminars, the keynote addresses and the Bible studies all added to the wealth of the conference, as did the stalls from various organizations, providing me with a fund of information to draw on in the future. There was no part of the week I would say was a waste of time. Perhaps more focus could have been given to learning the lessons of the past ten years, though to some extent that was done in the constituencies before the conference.

In common with other non-Anglicans at the conference, I felt privileged to be a part. It was good to meet with other Christians working with similar congregations, asking similar questions, facing similar restraints of finance and church structure to us, and to share ideas of how to share our faith with those who have not yet heard the Good News of Jesus Christ. Had I written this straight after the conference, it would have been full of enthusiasm, drawing on clearer memories, but Easter has been and gone since then. Now I look back on that week in March with a cooler appraisal – but still much enthusiasm.

Ruth Lackenby

Youth delegate from Durham Diocese

It was a cold but bright day as we approached the Hayes Conference Centre in Swanwick – for me it was the second visit in a relatively short space of time because in 1998 this had been the venue for the Durham Diocese Consultation. So I did have a little bit of an idea what to expect, from the venue at least.

In the run-up to ACE '99 I had met with the other delegates from Durham Diocese a number of times to plan and affirm our approach to the conference. We had decided that we would not necessarily rely completely on the guidelines laid down in the pre-conference literature but would develop our own approach and understanding of evangelism. My involvement was very much from a young person's angle, and in the pre-conference meetings and at the conference itself I was determined to see that young people would not be just a part, but be a 'central' part of our thinking on evangelism and the future. This is one of the main reasons why we put forward the maxim: 'How can young people be heard if the church doesn't listen?' And it is with this phrase in mind that I look back to the events of ACE '99.

Once I arrived and settled in I found it most refreshing to be mixing with Anglicans from so many different traditions and backgrounds. This is surely one of the great things about being an Anglican – diversity. But as I mixed with all these other Christians one question leapt out, 'where were all the young people?' There were over 300 delegates at the conference but there will not have been more than about 30 under the age of 30. Why should this be? Was it simply because younger people just did not want to take part? Had they not been asked? Had they not been taken seriously enough to have something to say at such a conference? Or had they not been listened to? Whatever the reason, youth was not well represented, and because of that the conference, I feel, lost out on an important dynamic.

As we met together in our Base Groups and Tracks what did become obvious was that some areas take the involvement of young people more seriously than others. Durham Diocese, the only diocese I can speak on with any personal knowledge may not have the best record when it comes to dealing with youth matters, but more and more Durham is now trying to see that young people are involved at the very heart of its thinking, urging involvement on both PCCs and synods. The bright note was that there did seem to be a growing awareness of the problem in the Church as a whole and ways were being sought to address the issue. ('Young people are not a problem – they are part of the answer.')

The Base Groups I attended I found very useful and here there was, in the main, an openness and frankness in our discussions which I found very refreshing. However, one of the problems was that some of the young people (and I suspect some of the older people as well), felt a little out of their depth. This was especially evident as in the bar in the evening the young people sat talking until the early hours of the morning, usually over a drink or two (non-alcoholic of course!) Here, away from the more academic and theological arguments of the day's meetings, we could all speak of the way we felt, the way God was speaking to each one of us. We could tell our own stories unafraid of what others might think. This is a problem; young people feel isolated sometimes because they feel they lack the necessary words to express themselves. However, if the Church takes time to listen, here will be found powerful testimony to the work of the Spirit in ordinary lives, all the more relevant because it comes from the heart and is not wrapped up in needless words.

As the conference progressed, I have to say how much I enjoyed the diversity offered in the way of worship. Both eucharistic and non-eucharistic services were enriched by their use of forms of service from other lands, even if some of the music tended to be very much the same. Maybe this is one way the worship could have been developed – by varying the music more. And as the conference progressed I think we all learned more about ourselves and just what evangelism means. Certainly I found both answers and new questions – but then that is the nature of these things.

So ACE '99 drew to its close, but not before some of the young people added a touch of excitement to the proceedings. It just so happened that Comic Relief's 'Red Nose' day fell during the conference and something had to be done to raise some money. So we kidnapped a bishop (the Bishop of Wakefield to be precise) and held him for ransom, and in so doing raised well over one thousand pounds. But then is not this also part of our commitment and our call – our care for all God's people? My part in the kidnap was carried out dressed as an angel, the Angel of the North (well I am from Gateshead). Because of this, when I spoke at the plenary session I was asked to stay 'in costume'. This must have been some sight.

ACE '99 has gone, but it is more than a memory. Through it I have made new friends all over the world (I have just received a letter from Bishop Henri of Uganda), and for me it has become a starting point, a launch pad for all sorts of exciting opportunities. I now question my own future and ask what God is calling me to. The answer lies somewhere in the stillness.

Stephen Cottrell

Missioner with Springboard

Ace – first or last?

In a deck of cards the ace is a paradoxical card. It is the lowest – a one – yet it outscores the highest – a king. For me the ACE conference on evangelism contained similar paradoxes. That it happened at all was marvellous. Many people, especially lay delegates from many dioceses, went home instructed and inspired. But when it came to one of its stated aims – to learn lessons from the Decade of Evangelism and plan for the future – little discernible progress was made. Take the ubiquitous Alpha course; whether you love it or loathe it, it bestrides the Decade. It is used in thousands of parishes and has been the way into evangelism for many. Its arrival in the Decade is part of a much wider rediscovery of the cate-chumenate and the development of a more holistic approach to evangelism which links the insights of faith development, educational methodology and liturgical renewal. Thus the Decade of Evangelism has been instrumental in encouraging a model of evangelism whose emphasis is on an accompanied journey leading beyond conversion to the full bap-tismal calling of the apostolic life. Yet Alpha itself received barely a mention at the conference, still less a critical appraisal. And this rediscov-ery of catechumenal methods of evangelism and discipleship – far and away the most significant blessing of the Decade – was also not dealt with outside of the Tracks. Thus my own estimation is that the Tracks and Base Groups were very helpful, but the main sessions rather a disappointment. They did not deal much with what we have learned about evangelism, but nor did they give a much needed theological perspective. Too many of the speakers emphasized the need for church culture to change, and for us to find ways of clothing the gospel in the cultures of our society. This is undoubtedly important, but there was little talk about the gospel itself. Yet if we are to be effective in evangelism we cannot avoid the question of truth. We need to ask 'What truth are we telling' and not just 'How do we tell it?' These truth issues – salvation, hell, homosexuality, remarriage, other faiths – are everyday issues for the local church. They have to be grappled with if we are to be effective in evangelism. Many people are alienated from the Church not because of our outdated culture, but because of what is perceived as our exclusive theologies. My hope is that in the next decade those of us who are motivated to share the gospel will dare extend the discussion on culture to include a discussion on gospel.

Ironically, the conference seemed to fall into the same trap that is my chief anxiety about the Alpha course; i.e. the Christian gospel is a closed book, rather than a story to be continued. But outside the Base Groups and the bar such a discussion, which may have opened up serious disagreements, was off limits. John Drane came closest to addressing this, but where he ended his talks is where I would have liked to begin – another paradox.

All this sounds rather negative when in fact I do not feel negative about the conference. It was a bit long (the alarm on my conference body clock starts ringing after 48 hours!) but there was a lot that was splendid. We missed an opportunity to celebrate and examine the astonishing phenomena of the renewal of the catechumenate – Alpha, Emmaus, Missionary Congregations and the rest – and like the rest of the Church of England we were scared stiff of theological discussion lest it should lead to disagreement. (And by the way the job of assessing the Decade still needs to be done. Who is going to write the report? This is an urgent need in my view.) But in the Tracks, in much of the worship, in the large numbers attending, there was a delightful realization that at last a demon had been cast out and that the Church of England was no longer frightened of the word 'evangelism'. We could own it as part of what it is to be Anglican. This in itself is a magnificent achievement – you might even call it ace! – and we needed a conference like this to chart how far we have travelled. And those who enabled the conference to happen deserve the heartfelt thanks of all the Church. Now we need to be bolder, teaching the lessons of the Decade in terms of method and culture, but daring to debate the questions of truth, which are at the centre of the good news.

Alan Stanley

Lay delegate from Ripon Diocese

'Wonderful to be greeted by Janice Price by name as I arrived, even before I had my name badge pinned on. I've only met Janice once before two or three years ago, and she remembered!' These were the opening words of the journal I kept through the conference. As I read through my impressions months later, some things have taken on deeper meaning, others have faded away. Janice's greeting, for example, has come to encapsulate all that ACE meant to me. Evangelism is personal, flowing from God who personally sent His Son, and coming to us through the love and care of individual Christians. So what sort of picture can I sketch of my impressions of ACE '99?

Background impressions

Warm fellowship – I moved from feeling isolated and alone during the first tea break to not having enough time for conversations by the final coffee time.

Missed opportunities – Did we really reflect on the Decade of Evangelism? Why was I disappointed with the archbishop's keynote address? Why was there not someone like Michael Green, surely one of the foremost theologians and practitioners of evangelism of today, speaking from the platform? Could we have achieved something more specific during the week?

Middleground impressions

People – what a lot of gifted people there are in the Church! In my Base Group we had people who are working with the Lord in so many interesting, challenging and stimulating ways. I had not heard Bishop Lindsay Urwin before. I would like to hear him again. The youth chaplain I shared a table with on the first evening was so in tune with his young people, it was just fascinating watching him. People definitely created a 'hope full' impression.

Foreground impressions

The most useful part of the conference for me was the Track on Transforming the Church in Mission. I have heard and read Robert Warren many times, and continue to learn from his gentle and authoritative words. Listening to what happened in other Tracks I suspect that for many these made the conference. I took a Special Interest Seminar on evangelistic preaching. Daniel Cozens would not, to be frank, be my choice of tutor. But I took his words to heart and on the following Sunday I preached as Daniel suggested, and had six enquirers after the service!

ACE '99 is not just about impressions. There has to be some analysis of the time and energy expended against the value of the exercise, and some attempt at discerning where the Spirit is leading. In other words a little reflection.

Value for time

The preparatory material was a joy to work through with the small group from my diocese. We saw how people come to faith in our area. Indeed we came to see that people come to faith in the most unlikely churches ! The preparation was well worth the time invested.

Reflecting on the time spent at the conference I picture it as my personal retreat in the market place. I was able to spend time in silence, time in corporate worship and Bible study and time in theological thinking in an environment of fellowship in the gospel. On a personal level this was time well spent.

Value for energy

I had nothing to do with the planning or running of the conference. Clearly the planning group members had invested considerable energy in ACE '99. Was the week worth that investment ? When the New Testament writer to the Hebrews told them not to neglect meeting together, the word used carries the meaning of an official assembly. The reason for meeting is given as encouraging one another, the idea is that Christians should strengthen and stimulate one another. There is a wonderful and intangible benefit from sharing with Christian sisters and brothers from different areas and different backgrounds. This benefit may not be noticed by the individual, only by those to whom he or she returns. This conference delegate certainly came home strengthened and stimulated. So, yes, definitely value for energy.

Where is the Spirit leading?

I wonder if openness is the word to ponder.

Openness to learn at the conference, openness to receive from people I would not naturally look to for advice and counsel, openness, as Bishop Nigel pointed out, to the renewing presence of the Holy Spirit.

There is one last openness, one abiding reflection of hope and joy. The young people were so vibrant and enthusiastic in their faith that this middle-aged Christian found, to his surprise, that he was 'enthusiastically challenged'. Are these young people the angels to the churches today – I want to listen to what the Spirit is saying through them!

5

Pointing to the Future

A Challenge to Action

ACE '99 was a conference of great contrasts and variety. It was a micro-cosm of the Church as we approach the end of the second Millennium. The variety was there in the wide range of theological perspectives repre-sented, in the approaches to worship, in age, colour, gender and denomination. That this conference attracted such a wide variety of people is perhaps indicative in itself of the success of the Decade of Evangelism. One participant commented that at the beginning of the Decade such a conference would have attracted only the evangelism enthusiasts but as the Decade draws to a close many more groups within the Churches were represented and are seeing evangelism much higher on their agendas. There was a high degree of theological dialogue in the Base Groups and Tracks as well as the countless informal discussions.

If variety was a strength of ACE '99 it also, perhaps, proved to be its limi-tation. There were those who departed the conference concerned that it did not come up with a clear direction for evangelism into the future. Or because ACE '99 had not sufficiently reflected upon the lessons learnt in the Decade of Evangelism. Both of these criticisms are fair. However, what was evident at ACE '99 were certain conflicts and tensions in approaches to evangelism which prevented the development of one clear voice from the conference. Perhaps it is that as the cultures to which the Churches seek to relate, and indeed are a part of, undergo rapid and unrelenting change which appear so often as a mass of conflicting voices, so the Churches too have to live with this same confusion. Is it this that we find so difficult? The aim of ACE '99 was to reflect on the lessons learnt from the Decade of Evangelism and to envision and enable the Churches to do evangelism into the new millennium. It is clear from conversations, evalu-ation forms and letters that many who attended were clearly enabled and envisioned for the work of evangelism. The process now moves to the ongoing reflection and evaluation of lessons learnt from the Decade of Evangelism among the Churches as a whole. ACE '99 began a process of necessary analysis and reflection which will go on for some time. This will involve the Churches as a whole and not just one conference.

The responsibility for the ongoing process beyond ACE '99 lies with the Mission, Evangelism and Renewal in England Committee (MERE), a Committee of the General Synod Board of Mission. MERE is keen to hear from people at all levels in the Churches about what has been learnt during the Decade of Evangelism, and to hear particular stories.

They can be contacted at the following address: Board of Mission, Church House, Great Smith Street, London SW1P 3NZ.

What were some of the tensions evident in ACE '99? First there was the tension between varying methods of evangelism. The attention of the conference was very particularly on the 'how' of doing evangelism. There was little examination of the content of the message we present and of the theological presuppositions we carry into evangelism. There was no examination of the relationship between method and content. In other words, what message are we presenting and how does that affect the means of presentation? Plans are already being made for a further conference to focus on the theology of evangelism in 2001.

Secondly, there was the tension surrounding the language of evangelism and the nature of the gospel.

Paul Vallely concluded his keynote address with the challenge:

> Ours is a people which does not, any longer, speak your language. Can you learn theirs?

For some the reply is clearly that we do need to learn the language of the cultures of which we are a part as well as being faithful to the Scriptures and tradition which form our identity as Christians. For others the need to learn a new language is a secondary concern. The primary concern being to get the gospel proclaimed. For yet others there is a clear need for both the content and the method of evangelism to change with the prevailing culture. All strands of thought were represented at ACE '99. However, despite the different theological perspectives there was clear convergence in the belief that evangelism is about risk. It is about sailing close to the wind. There was no better example of this than in John and Olive Drane's description of using Tarot cards in evangelism. They showed the rich biblical imagery in the cards and told stories of how they can be used to speak to people interested in the New Age. The context for this was a Bible Reading on Acts 17. The question is whether we are prepared to take risks in evangelism realizing that where there is risk there is cost.

The third identifiable tension at ACE '99 concerned relationships with church structures. There was a clear tension between the expectations of those who are part of the church structures for whom analysis of the Decade of Evangelism as a working concept is essential, and those who feel distant from church structures and for whom the Decade of Evangelism is a concept they are not familiar with. For this latter group it is evangelism in the here and now that matters. The results from the ACE '99 Evaluation Forms show a frustration by some that analysis of the

Decade was not more clearly focused in the programme. However, it is questionable whether such a large conference could have achieved any significant and lasting analysis. For others this may have appeared to look like endless navel-gazing while the key issues were the equipping and enabling for evangelism into the new millennium. From anecdotal evidence it is clear that the Decade of Evangelism has played a major role in getting evangelism into the thinking of the Churches. It has enabled discussion of evangelism by people and groups for whom it had previously been an area which was the exclusive domain of evangelicals. The wide range of theological perspectives present amongst those who attended ACE '99 is one indicator that evangelism has become the work of the whole Church.

The fourth tension evident at ACE '99 was that of generation. To some ACE '99 was a post-modern conference. One delegate (in their forties) remarked on the Service of Blessing – worship without words – and the themes of the Tracks as very postmodern. It was unclear what this meant but it showed that to them it looked and felt different to traditional style conferences. However, other younger delegates found ACE '99 just like a typical church conference with some important differences. On further questioning they meant that it comprised mostly older men speaking from the front, but again with important exceptions such as the Service of Blessing and Tracks on Information Technology and Storytelling. This reveals an important generational difference – that the world and the Church look different to differing generations and cultures. What ACE '99 sought to do was to listen to the many voices and the tensions that that difference creates and allow space for them to be heard. The extent to which this was achieved varied.

ACE '99 Resolutions

Although the process of ACE '99 did not specifically seek to make declarations and pass resolutions, two issues emerged from the conference that required a clear indication of conference opinion to form a basis for future action. These were the call for the establishment of a fund specifically for youth evangelism and for a research project into how people come to faith at the turn of the Millennium.

Conference delegates voted overwhelmingly for the following resolution:

That a fund be set up for new initiatives in *evangelism among young people*. This could be administered much in the same way as the Church Urban Fund. It would need to be ongoing in the Church's budget. We suggest £1 million would be a good start.

This resolution reflected the high degree of concern about the importance of evangelism among young people. Subsequent consultation has shown this to be true far beyond ACE '99. At the time of writing the responsibility for furthering this resolution rests with the Board of Mission in conjunction with the Board of Education.

The second resolution concerned the need for *research into the effectiveness of evangelism during the* 1990s. The resolution reads:

That this conference asks the Board of Mission and Churches Together in England to commission new research on the effectiveness of evangelism during the 1990s with a view to enhancing the planning and resourcing of the Church's mission in the twenty-first century.

Both the Board of Mission and the Group for Evangelization of Churches Together in England are responsible for the processing of this resolution. At the time of writing discussions are taking place between the two bodies and a theological college where the research may be conducted. It is generally agreed that this work would assist the development of evangelism beyond the Decade.

ACE '99 – A List of Issues Arising: A Personal Compilation

Philip King

Introduction

ACE '99 is a process that began with discussion in, and feedback from, the dioceses, mission agencies and groups before the conference. It will continue with reflection and action afterwards; the conference itself was a peak in, but not the culmination of the process. We deliberately avoided any simplistic summaries on the last day. This may have left some disoriented, especially those who are used to conferences that spend their time discussing and voting on resolutions prepared in advance. Again the range of people present meant that some issues and ideas were completely new to some and not to others; a conference of this kind is rightly a series of snapshots of developing processes, rather than heralding a complete break with the past and a total change of direction.

One of the problems of cataloguing the issues arising so far, both from the conference and from the preparatory material from dioceses and others, is that the cake can be cut several ways. One alternative approach to the one used below would be to catalogue by particular sector groups – e.g. children, youth, thirties to fifties, men, women, the poor. The reason why this approach has not been used is not that they are not important – far from it – but that the data is readily available in the track reports. Again we could subdivide the issues into theological or missiological and practical, or into message and method, but Marshall McLuhan was right in saying that 'the medium is the message', e.g. a monologue approach in teaching or evangelism can convey the message that the speaker is the only one with expertise and that there is nothing to be learnt from the experience and ideas of those present. In what follows it is assumed that theological reflection, experience and practice will all be involved, though in differing degrees, even where the question seems to be framed in theological terms.

Some of the lessons of the Decade

The briefest of lists will suffice here (taken from the summary of replies from dioceses). A fuller exposition can be found in Robert Warren's *Signs of Life: How Goes the Decade of Evangelism* (Church House Publishing, London, 1996, £4.95).

1. A major shift in how evangelism is perceived – good news is now on agendas, if not on lips; evangelism is no longer a completely negative concept.

2. Process and not just event; emphasis on the journey.

3. Relationships are key.

4. Spirituality must be central.

5. Evangelism cannot be separated from ministry, worship, and theology.

6. A variety of approaches are needed.

7. Action and proclamation must come together.

8. Evangelism can be tough – it needs patience and evaluation.

Two key phrases

Two key phrases stand out from the material –

Being 'faithful to the God who is always in mission.'
(The Archbishop of Canterbury)

'Spirit filled incarnational evangelism.'

The word 'God' in the first phrase can be expounded to refer to the Trinity; relationships, communication and mission are central to the Godhead.

A list of issues

Many of these issues are not new and in various forms can be found in the New Testament, but ACE '99 highlighted areas where further study, theological reflection and practical application and engagement are needed. Three steps that are relevant to most issues are to

Discover (what is happening)

Evaluate

Network (i.e. publicize and commend)

A. *A clearer understanding of the nature of our society*

   Local, national and global, at the beginning of the new millennium.

1. Clarifying the aspects of modernism and postmodernism that are currently affecting evangelism and the implications for our thinking and practice.

2. What are the other gods (Acts 17) that are being worshipped? (Dranes)

    What are people seeking for, and where?

    How can we learn their language? (Dranes/Vallely)

3. The implications for other sections below.

B. *What is the good news?*

> *For people in twenty-first century England – addressing the spiritual search of men and women today (Dranes/Vallely).*

4. How far is the issue simply one of presentation and how far should the gospel take different forms and shapes in different cultures and contexts?

5. What is the good news for the poor, for children, for youth, for women, for men and for other categories mentioned in the tracks and seminars?

6. Finding ways to share good news that are holistic, dealing with the transformation of society as well as individuals and exploring new ways of being (Isaiah 11 – Dranes).

C. *What is Church?*

> *New ways of being church for today; new wine skins; centred on the world.*

7. Making the church a learning organization – learning from other cultures and contexts, from the world Church and from different sociological, gender and ethnic contexts.

8. What should our new wine skins look like? What is the appropriate way of being church in our contemporary cultures and contexts?

    Comparing our different understandings of church (ecclesiologies)

    The implications of congregations becoming incarnated in their local culture and context; what does this mean in terms of shape, style, location, culture, etc.? (Much mention was made of the cultural divide and the resulting barriers.)

What are the implications of living in dispersed as well as gathered mode? (Monday to Saturday as well as Sunday)

How far is the Cell mode (geographical, network, community, work-based) appropriate as well as congregational and celebration modes?

The task of developing a missionary ecclesiology and crossing the divide between mission theology and faith and order groups.

9. What is essentially Anglican?

Other issues in section C:

10. The task of ensuring that evangelism stays central to the Church's thinking and life (the danger of saying 'we've done the Decade of Evangelism').

11. How far should church membership be open and how far bounded, how far defined and different without being exclusive; is there a proper difference in urban and rural contexts?

12. The relationship of believing and belonging; how can we make belonging easier?

13. What can we learn from Roman Catholics about the problems that arise when we separate evangelism from the church?

14. How best to develop ecumenical and other partnerships (e.g. deanery partnerships) in ways that promote rather than hinder evangelism (in this and other sections).

15. Discovering effective ways of tackling the burden of old church buildings.

16. Equipping each other for the development of deeper relationships both inside and outside the Church.

17. What forms of radical discipleship should we be teaching/demonstrating?

18. How can we achieve the strategic redirection of resources?

19. The particular contexts of smaller (and larger) churches.

D.   What is evangelism?

Examining afresh our understanding and application.

20.   The need to examine different theologies of evangelism:

What is the aim of evangelism?

What is the theology of the lost?

Should we emphasize kingdom theology or church theology?

Can social action in the orbit of Christian mission be called evangelism?

21.   Discovering, developing and sharing good models of community ministry/community involvement, combining social action, prophetic challenge, worship, discipleship and faith sharing – 'making new patterns for our community' (Dranes).

22.   Discovering, developing and sharing helpful examples of 'risk taking', cross-cultural evangelism, and witness to those of other faiths.

23.   Exploring the appropriate relationship of evangelism to spirituality, teaching, Christian community life, etc. Making evangelism a dimension, not a department, of church life. Learning from the Orthodox churches.

24.   Using the different approaches or channels of dialogue, proclamation, storytelling, mystery, signs, wonder, the arts, IT, and the media.

25.   Exploring the relationship of process and event.

E.   The agents of evangelism

The Holy Spirit working within and through the whole people of God.

26.   The need to affirm, enhance, share and evaluate the work of the evangelist.

27.   Equipping bishops, clergy and laity in effective leadership and evangelism

including issues of incarnation, relationships, dialogue and faith sharing

Finding, training, using mission enablers.

Looking afresh at ministerial training and adult education; equipping for collaborative leadership and engagement.

Index